A Dictionary of

COLORFUL ITALIAN IDIOMS

A Dictionary of
COLORFUL
ITALIAN IDIOMS

A TREASURY OF EXPRESSIONS

MOST COMMONLY FOUND IN

ITALIAN SPEECH AND

WRITING TODAY, WITH THEIR

AMERICAN EQUIVALENTS

Carla Pekelis
SARAH LAWRENCE COLLEGE

Illustrated by Paola Mazzetti

GEORGE BRAZILLER · *New York*

Preface

No collection of Italian idiomatic expressions can claim to be truly complete and exhaustive, so great is the variety available. I have attempted to select the forms most commonly found in Italian speech and writing, but I am aware that any choice of this kind must be, to a certain degree, arbitrary.

The expressions are listed under focal nouns and adjectives, only occasionally under a verb. Whenever an expression contains two nouns, it is listed under both entries.

Instead of using conventional signs to indicate genders, the definite article has been inserted, in the belief that the language student better absorbs noun and article as a unit. Most expressions are followed by an idiomatic translation or English equivalent and then by a literal word-for word translation. Whenever necessary, an example has been added. To further clarify Italian usage, such examples at times contain translations quite appropriate in the specific instances, yet different from the one or ones quoted immediately after the Italian expression.

By and large, proverbs have been omitted, partly because there are so many that they would require a separate book, partly because most of them have become clichés. Some, however, are so much a part of Italian thought that they are

constantly referred to in snatches. Others seem to have kept
their sting in spite of constant use. Still others have a bitter-
sweet Italian flavor, or an exact American counterpart. This is
why a few did creep back into the collection, almost against
my better judgment.

It is beyond the scope of this book to try to come to
conclusions of either a psychological or a social nature. The
attentive and imaginative reader may wonder about the
recurrence of expressions reflecting impatient, dramatic, good-
humored, and ironical moods. He may notice that the earthiness of such expressions as *"voler la botte piena e la moglie
ubriaca"* differs from the earthiness of their American counter-
parts. To such a reader I wish luck and dedicate the book.

My deepest thanks to Danielle Siena and Carl Rau-
shenbush who so generously gave of their time and advice.

C. P.

A Dictionary of

COLORFUL ITALIAN IDIOMS

A

ACCIDENTE (**L'**) Accident, mishap, stroke

Accidenti: Darn it! Damn!

Essere un accidente: To be quite a handful (said of a child); to be a powerhouse (said of an adult).

ACQUA (**L'**) Water

Acqua in bocca (See also **Mosca**): Mum's the word! Button your lip!
LIT. Water in your mouth.

Acqua passata non macina più: The past is the past, it's all water over the dam.
LIT. Past water no longer grinds.

Affogare in un bicchier d'acqua: To be easily put off by difficulties.
LIT. To drown in a glass of water.

Io non darei l'incarico a lei. Lo sai che quella *affoga in un bicchier d'acqua.* (I wouldn't give the assignment to her. You know how flustered she gets over nothing.)

All'acqua ci scalzeremo: We'll cross our bridges when we come to them.
LIT. At the water we'll take off our shoes.

Aver l'acqua alla gola: To be in trouble up to one's neck.
LIT. To have the water at one's throat.

Lo so anch'io che sarebbe un passo molto opportuno, ma vedrai che non si deciderà a compierlo finché non *avrà l'acqua alla gola.* (I agree that it would be a wise move on his part, but I'm sure he won't decide to act until he has absolutely no way out.)

Della più bell'acqua: Of the first water.
LIT. Of the most beautiful water.

Essere in cattive acque, navigare in cattive acque: To be in deep water, in bad trouble.
LIT. To be in bad waters, to sail in bad waters.

Fare acqua: Not to hold water, to be full of holes (said of a point of view).
·LIT. To make water, to leak.

Mi dispiace, ma il tuo ragionamento *fa acqua.* (I'm sorry, but your argument doesn't hold water.)

Fare un buco nell'acqua: To fail in an attempt, to get no place.
LIT. To make a hole in the water.

Ho cercato di persuadere X a imprestarmi il denaro, ma *ho fatto un buco nell'acqua.* (I tried to talk X into lending me the money, but I got absolutely nowhere.)

*Fare un buco nell'*acqua

Far venire l'acquolina in bocca: To make one's mouth water.
LIT. To make the little water come to one's mouth.

L'acqua cheta rovina i ponti: Still waters run deep.
LIT. Quiet water damages bridges.

Lasciar correre l'acqua per la sua china: To let things work themselves out; take their own course.
LIT. To let the water run along its slope.

Metter acqua nel proprio vino (See **Vino**)

Pestar l'acqua nel mortaio: To waste time and effort in an absurd pursuit.
LIT. To pound the water in the mortar.

> Non capisci che lui parla una lingua diversa dalla nostra, e che cercare di fargli vedere ragione è *pestar l'acqua nel mortaio?* (Don't you understand that he doesn't think the way we do, and trying to make him see the light is an absolute waste of time?)

Portare acqua al mare: (See also **portare Vasi a Samo**): To bring coals to Newcastle.
LIT. To bring water to the sea.

Stupido come l'acqua calda: As dull as dish water.
LIT. Stupid as warm water.

Una tempesta in un bicchier d'acqua: A tempest in a teapot.
LIT. A tempest in a glass of water.

Tirar l'acqua al proprio mulino: To be out for oneself.
LIT. To draw the water to one's own mill.

> Se fossi te, non mi fiderei troppo di lui. Quello è un tipo che *tira l'acqua al suo mulino.* (I wouldn't trust him too much if I were you. He only looks out for number one!)

AGO (L') Needle

Cercar l'ago nel pagliaio: To look for a needle in a haystack.

ALA (L') Wing

Avere le ali ai piedi, mettere le ali ai piedi: To run fast and eagerly; to have wings on one's heels.
LIT. To have wings at one's feet; to put wings at one's feet.

Fare ala: To make way respectfully for someone (said of a crowd or group of people).
LIT. To make wing.

Tarpare le ali a qualcuno: To clip someone's wings.

ALLORO (L') Laurel

Riposare sugli allori: To rest on one's laurels.

Scoprire gli altarini

ALTARE (L') Altar

Scoprire gli altarini: To stumble upon a friend's secrets or small indiscretions (said teasingly rather than accusingly).
LIT. To uncover the little altars.

Ah, è questo che venivi a fare in città il mercoledì. Bene, bene, *si scoprono gli altarini!* (So this is what you've been doing in town on Wednesdays . . . Well, what do you know!)

ALTEZZA (L') Height

Essere all'altezza (di): To be up to; to rise to the occasion.
LIT. To be at the height (of).

È stato un bel concerto, ma il soprano *non mi è parso all'altezza.* (It was a good concert, but I don't think the soprano was quite up to par.)

ALTO Tall, high, up

Far cascare qualcosa dall'alto: To give reluctantly or condescendingly, exaggerating the difficulties involved.
LIT. To let something fall from up high.

Chiedere un favore a lui? No davvero! *Li fa sempre cascare talmente dall'alto.* (Ask him for a favor? Not on your life! He always makes such a production out of it.)

Fare un alto là: To pull someone up short.
LIT. To make a halt.

Guardare qualcuno dall'alto in basso: To look down one's nose at someone.
LIT. To look at someone from high to low.

ALZATA (**L'**) Raising, rising, lifting up

Alzata d'ingegno: Brilliant idea (sarcastic).
LIT. Raising of talent.

Alzata di scudi (See also **Levata di scudi**): Sudden protest or act of rebellion.
LIT. Raising of shields.

Alzata di testa (See also **colpo di Testa**): Rash act.
LIT. Raising of head.

Fare un'alzataccia (See also **fare una Levataccia**): To get up at an ungodly hour.
LIT. To make an awful rising.

Fare un'alzataccia a qualcuno (See also **fare una Levataccia a qualcuno**): To jump down someone's throat.
LIT. To make an awful rising at someone.

AMBASCIATORE (**L'**) Ambassador

Ambasciator non porta pena: Ambassador carries no punishment.

Non ti arrabbiare! *Ambasciator non porta pena!* Io non faccio che trasmetterti le sue parole. (Take it easy! I'm just giving you the message as it was given to me. I'm not responsible for the contents.)

AMERICA (L')

Non ha scoperto l'America (See also **non ha inventato la Polvere**): He's no great shakes; he'll never set the world on fire.
LIT. He has not discovered America.

AMICIZIA (L') Friendship

Patti chiari, amicizia lunga.
LIT. Clear agreements, long friendship.

Senti, mio caro, *patti chiari* . . . io ti accompagno alla fermata dell'autobus, ma non credere che ti porti a casa in macchina! (Listen, dear, let's get one thing straight right now. I'll take you as far as the bus stop, but don't think I'm going to drive you all the way home!)

AMICO (L') Friend

Amici per la pelle: Bosom friends.
LIT. Friends by the skin.

Dagli amici mi guardi Iddio, ché dai nemici mi guardo io: With friends like these, who needs enemies!
LIT. May God protect me from my friends, for I can take care of my enemies.

Un vero amico si conosce nel bisogno: A friend in need is a friend indeed.
LIT. One knows one's true friend in need.

AMORE (L') Love

Amor proprio: A combination of pride, sense of responsibility, and a desire for perfection.
LIT. One's own love.

Rassegnati a dare un esame un po' meno brillante, e riposati questo weekend. *Hai troppo amor proprio,* e rischi di rovinarti la salute. (What if your exam is a little less brilliant! You expect too much of yourself. If you don't take the weekend off, you'll end up with a nervous breakdown.)

D'amore e d'accordo: In perfect harmony.
LIT. In love and agreement.

ANCORA (L') Anchor

L'ancora di salvezza: Life saver; last hope.
LIT. Anchor of safety.

Non so come ringraziarti, *sei la mia ancora di salvezza.* (I don't know how to thank you, you're really a life saver.)

ANDARE To go

A lungo andare: In the long run.
LIT. In long going.

Andare a Canossa*: To eat crow; to eat humble pie.
LIT. To go to Canossa.

Andare a genio, andare a fagiolo: To meet with someone's liking.
LIT. To go to someone's genius; to go to someone's bean.

Sarà una bravissima persona, ma c'è qualcosa in lui che *non mi va a genio.* (I'm sure he's a fine person, but there's something about him that rubs me the wrong way.) Quello è un ragazzo che *mi va proprio a genio.* (That's a young man after my own heart.)

Andare a ruba: To go like hot cakes; to be at a premium.
LIT. To go at a steal.

Guarda che quando suona X i biglietti *vanno sempre a ruba.* (Be careful, when X plays, tickets are always at a premium.)

---

* Referring to Henry IV's painful apologies to Pope Gregory VII.

/ 7

Andare a zonzo: To wander about; to loaf.
LIT. To go to "zonzo" (used only in this expression).

> Non ho visto né chiese né musei. *Sono semplicemente andato a zonzo per la città.* (I saw neither the churches nor the museums. I just wandered around the city.)

Andare da sé: To go without saying.
LIT. To go by itself.

Andare in brodo di giuggiole (See **Brodo**)

Andare in solluchero: To take great pleasure in something, to delight in it.
LIT. To go into mouth-watering.

> Le lodi *lo mandano in solluchero.* (He really thrives on praise.)

Andare in visibilio (See **Visibilio**)

Non andar giù: Not to be able to accept or to stomach something or someone; to stick in the throat.
LIT. Not to go down.

> Più ci penso, e più quel che ha detto *non mi va giù.* (The more I think of what he said, the more unforgivable I think it is.)

ANIMA (L') Soul

Anima gemella: Kindred spirit.
LIT. Twin soul.

Essere due anime in un nocciolo: To get along perfectly.
LIT. To be two souls in one pit.

Regger l'anima coi denti: To be in very poor health; to hold on to life by a thread.
LIT. To hold one's soul with one's teeth.

Rimetter l'anima in corpo a qualcuno: To reassure someone; to give him new hope and confidence.
LIT. To put back the soul in someone's body.

Che Dio ti benedica! Le notizie che mi hai dato *mi han rimesso l'anima in corpo.* (God bless you! What you just told me has given me a new lease on life!)

Rompere l'anima a qualcuno (See also **rompere le Scatole**): To exasperate someone; to be a pain in the neck.
LIT. To break someone's soul.

ANTIFONA (L') Antiphony

Capire l'antifona: To take the hint.
LIT. To understand the antiphony.

Ho capito l'antifona! Preferisci andarci solo. (Okay, I get the message. You'd rather go alone.)

APPARENZA (L') Appearance

Salvare le apparenze: For the sake of appearances.
LIT. To save appearances.

Mi dispiace d'insistere, ma credo sia importante *salvare le apparenze* continuando a vederlo di tanto in tanto. (I'm sorry to keep harping on it, but I think it's important to see him every once in a while for the sake of appearances.)

APPETITO (L') Appetite

Buon appetito: Enjoy your meal!
LIT. Good appetite (to you).

L'appetito vien mangiando: A taste of something (food, work, or pleasure) increases your desire for it.
LIT. Appetite comes through eating.

Stuzzicare l'appetito: To whet the appetite.

ARGENTO VIVO (L') Quicksilver

Aver l'argento vivo addosso: To be unable to keep still.
LIT. To have quicksilver on.

Non so come fai a tener dietro a quel bambino. *Ha proprio l'argento vivo addosso.* (I don't know how you keep up with that child. He doesn't sit still for a minute!)

ARIA (L') Air

Andare all'aria (See also **andare a Monte**): To fall through.
LIT. To go to the air.

La crociera? Tutto *all'aria!* (The cruise? It's all off!)

Aver la testa per aria, essere una testa per aria: To be absent-minded, forgetful.
LIT. To have one's head in the air; to be a head-in-the-air.

È una testa per aria di prim'ordine! (If he didn't have his head fastened on, he'd forget that too!)

Campato in aria: Groundless; without foundation.
LIT. Set in air.

È un progetto *campato in aria.* (It's an unrealistic plan:)

Darsi delle arie: To give oneself airs.

Darsi l'aria di: To want to give the impression of; to pose as.
LIT. To give oneself the air of.

Si dà l'aria di un conoscitore di musica. (He tries to give the impression that he's a musical expert.)

Far castelli in aria: To build castles in the air.

Mandare all'aria qualcosa (See also **mandare a Monte qualcosa**): To call something off in irritation or impatience.
LIT. To send something to the air.

ARMA (L') Weapon

Arma a doppio taglio: Double-edged sword; plan, idea that is likely to boomerang.
LIT. Double-edged weapon.

Stai attento, mi sembra che la tua sia *un'arma a doppio taglio.* (Be careful, you may well be hoist with your own petard.)

Con armi e bagagli: Bag and baggage.
LIT. With arms and baggage.

Essere alle prime armi: To be inexperienced; to be a novice in a given field.
LIT. To be at one's first arms.

Fare il viso dell'arme: To look alarmed and on the defensive upon hearing something.
LIT. To make the face of arms.

Con armi e bagagli

Non fare il viso dell'arme, ti prego. Nessuno vuol costringerti a partire tuo malgrado. (Don't get excited! Nobody is going to make you leave against your will.)

Sotto le armi: In the service (military).
LIT. Under the arms.

ARNESE (L') Tool

Cattivo arnese: Disreputable type, no-good.
LIT. Bad tool.

Male in arnese (See **Male**)

ARTE (L') Art

Non avere né arte né parte: To have neither a job nor any prospects.
LIT. To have neither art nor role.

Come si fa a prender moglie, quando *non si ha né arte né parte?* (How can one think of marriage without a job or a cent to one's name?)

ASCIUTTO Dry

Essere all'asciutto (See also **essere al Verde**): To be broke.
LIT. To be at the dry.

ASINO (L') Donkey, ass

Asino calzato e vestito: A perfect ass.
LIT. An ass with shoes and clothes on.

Essere l'asino di Buridano*: To be incapable of choosing, of making up one's mind.
LIT. To be Buridan's donkey.

Lavare la testa all'asino: To give assistance where it is neither solicited nor appreciated.
LIT. To wash the donkey's head.

Legar l'asino dove vuole il padrone: To follow orders, to do as one is told.
LIT. To tie the donkey where the master wants.

Lavare la testa all'asino

Meglio un asino vivo che un dottore morto: Better a live coward than a dead hero.
LIT. Better a live ass than a dead doctor.

Qui casca l'asino: That's the problem, the stumbling block.
LIT. Here falls the donkey.

Raglio d'asino non giunge in cielo: The voice of a fool doesn't carry very far.
LIT. The bray of a donkey doesn't reach heaven.

ASSO (L') Ace

Avere un asso nella manica: To have an ace up one's sleeve.

Essere un asso: To be an ace.

Piantare in asso qualcuno: To leave someone flat.
LIT. To plant (leave) someone in ace.

---

* In the story, attributed to the French philosopher Jean Buridan, the donkey—torn between two piles of hay—dies of hunger.

ATTO (L') Act

All'atto pratico: In practice.
LIT. At the practical act.

Fare atto di presenza: To put in an appearance.
LIT. To make an act of presence.

AVERE To have

Avercela con qualcuno: To be mad at someone.
LIT. To have it with someone.

> Non so perché, ma *ce l'ha con me.* (I don't know why, but I seem to be in the doghouse these days.)

Avercela a morte con qualcuno: To be bitterly resentful of someone.
LIT. To have it to death with someone.

AVVOCATO (L') Lawyer

Avvocato delle cause perse: Champion of lost causes.
LIT. Lawyer (specializing in) lost cases.

> Me l'aspettavo che avresti trovato qualche buona spiegazione per il suo comportamento. Il solito *avvocato delle cause perse!* (I knew you'd come up with some excuse for him! An optimist to the last!)

Far l'avvocato del diavolo, far la parte del diavolo: To be the devil's advocate.

B

BACCHETTA (LA) Stick, baton, wand

Comandare a bacchetta: To be an authoritarian; to order people around.
LIT. To command by stick.

> Se vedessi . . . ha appena cinque anni e ci *comanda tutti a bacchetta!* (You should see her . . . She's barely five and orders all of us around!)

BAFFO (IL) Mustache

Leccarsi i baffi: To lick one's chops.
LIT. To lick one's mustache.

Ridere sotto i baffi (See also **leccarsi le Labbra, le Dita**): To laugh up one's sleeve.
LIT. To laugh under one's mustache.

BALDORIA (LA) Bonfire

Far baldoria: To have a wild time, a ball.
LIT. To make a bonfire.

BALLO (IL) Ball, dance

Entrare in ballo: To come
into the picture.
LIT. To enter the dance.

> È inutile, quando *entrano
> in ballo* i quattrini . . .
> (When money comes into
> the picture, you might as
> well forget it.)

Essere in ballo: To be involved.
LIT. To be in the dance.

Entrare in ballo

Tirare in ballo qualcuno o qualcosa: To bring up something; to involve someone.
LIT. To draw into the dance someone or something.

> Fammi il piacere, *non tirare in ballo* la questione morale.
> (Let's keep the moral implications out of this, shall we?)
> Perché vuoi *tirare in ballo* me? Sono affari tuoi! (Why do
> you want to get me involved? It's your business.)

BANCO (IL) Bench, counter

Sordo come un banco (See **Sordo**)

Sotto banco: Under the counter; surreptitiously; on the side.

Tener banco: To hold court.
LIT. To hold counter (to be the dealer at a gambling table).

BANDOLO (IL) End (of a skein)

Trovare il bandolo della matassa: To find the clue to a situation, to a knotty problem.
LIT. To find the end of the skein.

BARACCA (LA) Hut, shack

Mandare avanti la baracca: To keep a business or a household going, no matter how precariously.
LIT. To push the hut along.

Mi hanno detto che è il vecchio padre a *mandare avanti la baracca*. (I'm told it's the old father who keeps things going.)

Piantare baracca *e burattini*

Piantare baracca e burattini: To walk out on a situation; to give something up lock, stock, and barrel.
LIT. To plant (leave) hut and puppets.

Ho una voglia pazza di *piantar baracca e burattini* e tornarmene a casa. (At this point, I'd love to go home and forget the whole thing.)

BARBA (LA) Beard

Aver la barba lunga (di una storia, una barzelletta): So old it's got whiskers.
LIT. To have a long beard (of a story, a joke).

Farla in barba a qualcuno: To succeed in the face of someone's determined opposition.
LIT. To do it at someone's beard.

Far venire la barba: To bore to death.
LIT. To make someone's beard grow.

Servire qualcuno di barba e di capelli: To give someone what's coming to him, his comeuppance.
LIT. To serve someone of beard and hair.

Non te la prendere! *L'ho servito di barba e di capelli.* (Don't worry, I fixed his wagon!)

BARCA (LA) Boat

Aiutare la barca: To pitch in; to help keep a family afloat.
LIT. To help the boat.

Tirare i remi in barca: To get ready for the conclusion (of a day, a deal, or life itself).
LIT. To draw the oars in the boat.

Mettermi in una nuova combinazione? Caro mio, alla mia età è tempo di pensare a *tirare i remi in barca.* (Me? At my age? It's time for me to call it a day, not to get involved in something new.)

BARILE (IL) Barrel

Fare a scaricabarile: To pass the buck.
LIT. To do (play) at unloading barrels.

Chi è stato? Vattelapesca! Quelli *fanno a scaricabarile.* (Who did it? God knows! They're all so busy passing the buck that it's hard to tell.)

Fare il pesce in barile (See **Pesce**)

BATTERE To beat, to strike

Battere il ferro finché è caldo: To strike while the iron is hot.

Battere in ritirata: To beat a retreat.
LIT. To beat in retreat.

Battere la fiacca: To do things sluggishly, lazily.
LIT. To strike indolence.

Sarebbe un buon impiegato, ma *batte un po' la fiacca.* (He has the makings of a good worker, but he doesn't care to exert himself too much.)

Battere la grancassa: To call attention ostentatiously to something; to beat the drum for something.
LIT. To beat the bass drum.

In un battibaleno: In a flash.
LIT. In one clap of lightning.

BECCO (IL) Beak

Ecco fatto il becco all'oca: There, the job is finished!
LIT. Here is made the goose's beak.

Mettere il becco a mollo: To drink.
LIT. To soak one's beak.

Ha sempre bisogno di tenere *il becco a mollo.* (He always has to have a glass in his hand.)

Mettere il becco in qualcosa: To interfere; to put in one's two cents' worth.
LIT. To put one's beak into something.

Vuol sempre *mettere il becco* nelle cose che non lo riguardano. (He always has to put in his two cents.)

Non avere il becco di un quattrino: To be absolutely penniless.
LIT. Not to have the beak of a farthing.

BELLEZZA (LA) Beauty

Che bellezza: How marvelous! How simply wonderful!
LIT. What beauty.

BELLO Beautiful

Bell'e buono: Real; out-and-out.

LIT. Beautiful and good.

> È un mascalzone *bell'e buono.* (He's an out-and-out scoundrel.)

C'è voluto del bello e del buono: To go to a lot of trouble.
LIT. It took some beautiful and good.

> *C'è voluto del bello e del buono* per convincerlo a partire. (It took a lot of persuading to get him to leave.)

Farsi bello con le penne del pavone: To dress in borrowed finery, to claim credit for other people's achievements.
LIT. To make oneself beautiful with the peacock's feathers.

> Non credo che sia merito suo e non mi meraviglierebbe

Farsi bello *con le penne del pavone*

che *si facesse bello con le penne del pavone.* (I doubt that he had anything to do with it. I wouldn't be surprised if he were simply taking the credit for someone else's work.)

Farsi bello del sol d'agosto: To take credit for events that are really beyond one's control.
LIT. To make oneself beautiful of the August sunshine.

Farsi bello di: To take the credit for.
LIT. To make oneself beautiful of.

Il bello è che: The beauty of it is that.
LIT. The beautiful is that.

Non è bello quel che è bello, è bello quel che piace: Beauty is in the eye of the beholder.
LIT. It's not what's beautiful that is beautiful, it's what one likes that is beautiful.

Raccontarne delle belle, sentirne delle belle: To have some pretty good ones to tell; to hear some pretty good ones.
LIT. To tell some beautiful ones; to hear some beautiful ones.

Scamparla bella: To have a narrow escape.
LIT. To escape a beautiful one.

Fortuna ch'eri uscito! È venuto X e ha chiesto di te. *L'hai scampata bella.* (You can thank your lucky stars that you had left! X came and asked about you. You really had a close call.)

Sul più bello: In the very midst of; at the crucial point.
LIT. On the most beautiful.

BENE Well

Ti sta bene: Serves you right.
LIT. It fits you well.

BENSERVITO (IL) Reference, recommendation

Dare il benservito: To dismiss, to fire, to give somebody the ax.
LIT. To give the good reference.

BERE To drink

Bere e zufolare (See also **voler la botte piena e la Moglie ubriaca**): To have your cake and eat it too.
LIT. To drink and to whistle.

Bere o affogare: It's either sink or swim.
LIT. To drink or to drown.

Darla a bere a qualcuno: To have someone believe something preposterous.
LIT. To give it to drink to someone.

Non me *la dai a bere!* (Don't expect me to swallow that!)

BERLINA (**LA**) Pillory, berlin (carriage)

Mettere alla berlina: To expose to public derision.
LIT. To put into the pillory.

BERNOCCOLO (**IL**) Bump

Avere il bernoccolo di: To have a knack for.
LIT. To have the bump of (as in phrenology).

BESTIA (**LA**) Beast, animal

Andare in bestia: To fly into a rage.
LIT. To go in beast.

Mandare in bestia qualcuno: To send someone into a rage; to give him a fit.
LIT. To send someone in beast.

BISOGNO (**IL**) Need

Il bisognino fa trottar la vecchia: Necessity is the mother of invention.
LIT. The little need makes the old woman trot.

Un vero amico si conosce nel bisogno (See **Amico**)

BOCCA (**LA**) Mouth

A mezza bocca (See also **a Fior di labbra**): Halfheartedly; unwillingly; perfunctorily.

LIT. At half mouth.

> Sì, mi ha invitato, ma *a mezza bocca*. (Yes, he did ask me, but without much conviction.)

Avere ancora il latte alla bocca: To be wet behind the ears.
LIT. To still have milk at one's mouth.

Aver la schiuma alla bocca: To foam at the mouth, to be beside oneself with rage.
LIT. To have the foam at one's mouth.

Chiudere la bocca a qualcuno: To silence someone with an irrefutable argument.
LIT. To close someone's mouth.

Di bocca in bocca: In the telling.
LIT. From mouth to mouth.

> Non ne parlare in giro, ti prego. *Di bocca in bocca* le cose cambiano. (Please don't repeat this to anyone. Things get so distorted as they are passed on.)

Essere di bocca buona: To be easy to please, not fussy.
LIT. To be of good mouth.

Essere la bocca della verità: To be truth itself.
LIT. To be the mouth of truth.

> Se lo dice lui, è senz'altro così. *È la bocca della verità.* (If he says so, that's the way it is. He's the soul of truth.)

Far boccuccia: To demur in a somewhat precious way.
LIT. To make little mouth.

In bocca al lupo (See **Lupo**)

Mettere bocca in qualcosa: To interfere; to offer an unsolicited opinion.
LIT. To put one's mouth into something.

> Scusami se *ci metto bocca,* ma mi sembra tu parta da una premessa sbagliata. (Forgive me for butting in, but I think you have your facts wrong.)

Non ricordarsi dal naso alla bocca: To have a bad memory (and not much brains).

LIT. Not to remember from one's nose to one's mouth.

Restare a bocca aperta (See also **restare di Sale**): To be left speechless, open-mouthed.
LIT. To be left with one's mouth open.

Restare a bocca asciutta: To be left without what one had hoped to get.
LIT. To remain with dry mouth.

> Quando finalmente è venuto il nostro turno, non c'erano più biglietti e *siamo rimasti a bocca asciutta*. (When our turn finally came the tickets were all gone, and we were left empty-handed.)

Riempirsi la bocca di: To brag about something; to indulge in self-pride.
LIT. To fill one's mouth with.

> *Si riempie la bocca* delle glorie di famiglia, ma intanto ha una posizioncina da nulla! (He loves to talk about his family's past to cover up the fact that his own achievements are negligible.)

Rifarsi la bocca: To try to forget the taste of bad food or of a bad experience with a new and satisfying one.
LIT. To remake one's mouth.

> Grazie della serata. Dopo un pomeriggio così estenuante, *mi son rifatto la bocca*. (Thank you for the wonderful evening. After such an exhausting afternoon it really put some life back into me.)

Storcere la bocca: To turn up one's nose.
LIT. To twist one's mouth.

BOCCONE (IL) Morsel, mouthful

A pezzi e bocconi: Piecemeal; in bits and pieces; in dribs and drabs.
LIT. By pieces and mouthfuls.

Boccone amaro: Bitter pill.
LIT. Bitter morsel.

Per un boccon di pane: For next to nothing, for peanuts.
LIT. For a morsel of bread.

Qualche anno fa si sarebbe potuto avere quella casa *per un boccon di pane*. (A few years ago, one could have bought that house for a song.)

Prendersela per il boccon della morte: To be bitterly offended by and resentful of someone's attitude.
LIT. To take it for the mouthful of death.

Scherzo o no, *se l'è presa per il boccon della morte*, e ha giurato di non rimetter piede in casa tua. (Joke or no joke, he took it very badly and swears he'll never set foot in your house again.)

BOLLETTA (LA) Little bubble, voucher

Essere in bolletta: To be short of money.
LIT. To be in voucher.

BOMBA (LA) Bomb

A prova di bomba: Bombproof; adamant; boundless.
Ha una pazienza *a prova di bomba*. (His patience knows no limits.)

Tornare a bomba: To get back to the subject.
LIT. To return to bomb.

BORDONE (IL) Bourdon, burden (musical)

Tener bordone a qualcuno: To help someone in an unworthy endeavor; to be in cahoots with someone.
LIT. To play the burden.

Non basta che lui faccia lo stupido! Ora ci sei tu a *tenergli bordone*. (It's bad enough that he behaves so foolishly without your egging him on!)

BORGHESE (IL) Bourgeois, civilian

In borghese: In mufti, in civvies.
LIT. In civilian.

BORSA (LA) Bag, purse

Stringere i cordoni della borsa: To tighten the purse-strings.

Tenere i cordoni della borsa: To hold the purse-strings.

BOTTA (LA) Blow, slap

A botta calda: Immediately; when the iron is hot.
LIT. At warm blow.

Rispondigli ora, *a botta calda,* e la lettera ti verrà più spontanea. (I think you'll do a better job if you answer him now, while you still feel so strongly about it.)

Botte da orbi: Violent, blind blows.
LIT. Blows such as blind people (would give).

Altro che se si son picchiati? Li avessi visti, *botte da orbi!* (Did they come to blows? You should have seen them, it was a regular free-for-all!)

BOTTE (LA) Barrel, cask

Dare un colpo al cerchio ed uno alla botte: To try to remain on good terms with both sides; to hunt with the hounds and run with the hare; to do two things at once.
LIT. To give one blow to the hoop and one to the cask.

Essere in una botte di ferro: To be quite confident of the invulnerability of one's line of action; to have an iron-clad case.
LIT. To be in an iron barrel.

Farmi causa? Impossibile! *Sono in una botte*

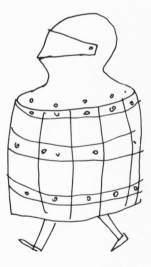

Essere in una botte di ferro

di ferro. (Sue me? Impossible! I'm completely covered.)

La botte dà il vino che ha: You can't make a silk purse out of a sow's ear.
LIT. The cask gives the wine it has.

Nelle botti piccole c'è il vino buono (See **Vino**)

Voler la botte piena e la moglie ubriaca (See **Moglie**)

BOTTEGA (LA) Shop

Fermarsi alla prima bottega: To settle for a less than perfect solution.
LIT. To stop at the first shop.

A parlarci sembrerebbe una persona competente, ma non voglio *fermarmi alla prima bottega,* e ho intenzione di vedere altre persone. (Judging from what he says, he seems competent enough, but I want to be sure I've really combed the field and I'm going to interview a few more people.)

Attaccare un bottone

BOTTONE (IL) Button

Abbottonato: Tight-lipped, reserved.
LIT. Buttoned up.

Attaccare un bottone: To buttonhole someone; to subject one to a long rambling discourse.
LIT. To attach (sew on) a button.

Sbottonarsi: To come out of one's reserve; to open up; to consent to reveal one's information or opinion on a matter.
LIT. To unbutton oneself.

Per farlo sbottonare, c'è voluta una serata intera. (It took me a whole evening to get him to speak his mind on the subject.)

BRACCIO (IL) Arm

A braccetto, sottobraccio: Arm in arm.
LIT. At little arm; under arm.

Avere le braccia legate (See also **avere le Mani legate**):
To have one's hands tied.
LIT. To have one's arms tied.

Avere le braccia lunghe: To be very influential.
LIT. To have long arms.

Essere il braccio destro di qualcuno: To be someone's right arm; right-hand man.

Sentirsi cascare le braccia: To lose heart; to feel utterly discouraged, frustrated.
LIT. To feel one's arms fall.

Quando ho saputo che aveva lasciato anche questo posto, *mi son sentito cascare le braccia.* (When I heard she had quit this job, too, I just gave up.)

Star con le braccia in croce: To sit doing nothing, with folded arms.
LIT. To stay with one's arms in a cross.

BRACA (LA) Trouser leg, trousers, pants

Calar le brache: To give in easily out of cowardice (rather crude).
LIT. To take one's pants down.

Se *ti cali le brache* alle prime minaccie, non arriveremo mai a nulla. (If you let them know you're scared, we'll never get what we want.)

BRECCIA (LA) Breach

Essere sulla breccia: To be active; to be in the thick of the fight.

LIT. To be on the breach.

> È un uomo meraviglioso. Quasi settant'anni e ancora *sulla breccia*. (He's an amazing person. Nearing seventy and still in there pitching!)

Far breccia: To make a deep impression on someone; to convince him; to talk him into something.
LIT. To make breach.

BREVE Short, brief

A farla breve: To make it short; to make a long story short.

BRODO (IL) Broth

Andare in brodo di giuggiole: To show delight in a very effusive way.
LIT. To go into a broth of berries.

> Ogni volta che si nomina suo figlio, *va in brodo di giuggiole*. (Every time her son is mentioned, she goes into ecstasies.)

Lamentarsi del brodo grasso: Not to know a good thing when one has it.
LIT. To complain of fat broth.

Lasciar cuocere qualcuno nel suo brodo: To let someone stew in his own juice.
LIT. To let someone cook in his broth.

Tutto fa brodo: Everything is grist to the mill.
LIT. Everything makes broth.

BUCCIA (LA) Peel, rind

Rivedere le bucce a qualcuno: To go over someone's work with rigorous criticism, with a fine-toothed comb.
LIT. To go over someone's peels.

BUCO (IL) Hole

Fare un buco nell'acqua (See **Acqua**)

Non sapere cavare un ragno da un buco: To be a do-nothing; to never be able to get anything done.
LIT. Not to know how to get a spider out of a hole.

> L'incarico a lui? Ma se non è capace di *cavare un ragno da un buco!* (Give *him* the assignment? He doesn't even know enough to come in out of the rain!)

Non tutte le ciambelle riescono col buco: Things cannot always work out according to plan.
LIT. Not all doughnuts come out with the hole.

Pezo el tacon del buso: The remedy is worse than the original ill.
LIT. (Venetian dialect for) The patch is worse than the hole.

> Non cercare di rimediare, ché è *pezo il tacon del buso.* (Don't try to cover up that faux pas. You're only making things worse.)

Tappare un buco: To pay off a debt.
LIT. To fill up a hole.

> Ma quei cinquecento dollari son serviti soltanto a *tappare qualche buco.* Il grosso è ancora da pagare. (True, those five hundred dollars helped me over some rough spots, but I'm not in the clear by any means.)

BUE (IL) Ox

Chiudere la stalla dopo che son fuggiti i buoi: To lock the barn door after the horse has been stolen.
LIT. To close the barn after the oxen have fled.

Mettere il carro avanti ai buoi: To put the cart before the horse.
LIT. To put the cart before the oxen.

Moglie e buoi dei paesi tuoi (See **Moglie**)

BUIO (IL) Darkness

Essere al buio: To be in the dark.

Fare un salto nel buio: To take a big chance.
LIT. To leap in the dark.

Tenere al buio qualcuno: To keep someone in the dark.

BUONO Good

Alla buona: Simply, informally, unpretentiously; simple, informal.
LIT. In the good (way).

> Vedrai che si tratta di gente *alla buona.* (You'll see, they're very easygoing, unpretentious people.)

Buono a nulla: Good-for-nothing, no good.

Buono come il pane (See **Pane**)

Mettercisi di buzzo buono: To put one's shoulder to the wheel.
LIT. To put oneself at it with good paunch.

> Ti assicuro che se *ti ci metti di buzzo buono,* stasera è finito. (If you really put your mind to it, I assure you you'll be done by tonight.)

Poco di buono: A no-good.
LIT. A little of good.

Prendere con le buone: To approach someone in a kind and persuasive way.
LIT. To take (someone) with good (manners).

> È un ragazzo dal quale si ottiene tutto, *se lo si prende con le buone.* (You can get that boy to do anything, if you go about it in the right way.)

C

CACIO (IL) Cheese

Alto come un soldo di cacio: Of small stature (said of children), knee-high.
LIT. As tall as a penny's worth of cheese.

Arrivare come il cacio sui maccheroni: To come in at just the right time.
LIT. To arrive like cheese on macaroni.

> Bravo, caschi proprio *come il cacio sui maccheroni!* Sei il perfetto arbitro in una discussione di questo tipo. (You're just the person we needed! The ideal referee in an argument of this type.)

Come il cacio sui maccheroni: Just about perfect.
LIT. Like cheese on macaroni.

Essere pane e cacio: To be close friends, lovey-dovey.
LIT. To be bread and cheese.

Altro che se puoi invitarli insieme! Son diventati *pane e cacio.* (Can you have them over together? I should say so, they've become inseparable.)

CAGNESCO Dog-like

Guardare in cagnesco: To look daggers at someone.
LIT. To look at someone in dog-like (way).

CAIO Caius (man's name)

Caio, Tizio o Sempronio: Tom, Dick or Harry.

CALCAGNO (IL) Heel

Stare alle calcagna di qualcuno: To be on someone's heels, to hound him.

CALDO Hot

Non mi fa né caldo né freddo: Doesn't affect me one way or another; I couldn't care less.
LIT. It doesn't do me either hot or cold.

CALENDE (LE) Calends

Rimandare alle calende greche: To postpone indefinitely.
LIT. To postpone till the Greek calends.

CALLO (IL) Callus

Fare il callo a qualcosa: To become inured to.
LIT. To make the callus to something.

Arrabbiarmi perché è in ritardo? Che vuoi, son venticinque anni che viviamo insieme. Ormai *ci ho fatto il callo.* (Get mad because she's late? We've been married twenty-five years, and I've learned to take it in my stride.)

CALZA (LA) Stocking

Fare le calze a qualcuno (See also **fare le Scarpe**): To inform on someone.
LIT. To make the stockings to somebody.

Farsi tirare le calze: To play hard-to-get.
LIT. To get someone to pull your stockings.

Mezza calzetta: Person of limited capacities.
LIT. Half a sock.

CAMICIA (LA) Shirt

Camicia di Nesso*: An unbearable moral predicament.
LIT. Nessus' shirt.

Ti assicuro che questo affare è per me *una vera camicia di Nesso.* (I tell you, this thing will be the end of me.)

Dimenticarsi di qualcosa come della prima camicia: To forget something utterly and completely.
LIT. To forget something as (one has forgotten) one's first shirt.

Nascere con la camicia

Nascere con la camicia: To be born lucky.
LIT. To be born with a shirt.

Sudar sette camicie: To put a great deal of effort into something.
LIT. To sweat seven shirts.

Mi ha fatto *sudar sette camicie,* ma finalmente si è convinto. (He gave me no end of trouble, but finally he came around to my point of view.)

---

* A shirt, imbued with the centaur Nessus' blood, which is said to have caused the death of Hercules.

CAMMINARE To walk

Camminare per (i cinquant'anni, i sessant'anni, ecc.): To be pushing (fifty, sixty, etc.).
LIT. To walk for the (fifty years, sixty years, etc.).

Camminare sulle uova: To walk on eggs.

Camminare su un filo di rasoio: To walk the razor's edge.

CAMPAGNA (LA) Countryside, campaign

Battere la campagna: To comb the district.
LIT. To beat the countryside.

Camminare *sulle uova*

Fare una campagna a favore di o contro qualcuno o qualcosa: To campaign for or against.
LIT. To make a campaign for or against someone or something.

Mettersi in campagna: To start working on something, to get busy.
LIT. To put oneself in campaign.

CAMPANA (LA) Bell

Sentire le due campane: To listen to both sides before forming an opinion.
LIT. To hear both bells.

Sordo come una campana (See **Sordo**)

Vivere sotto una campana di vetro: To lead a very careful life.
LIT. To live under a glass bell.

Ha avuto un attacco di cuore assai grave, e bisogna *viva*

sotto una campana di vetro. (He had a very bad heart attack and has to be extremely careful.)

CAMPO (IL) Field

Mettere il campo a rumore: To spread a piece of news and get people worked up on the issue involved.
LIT. To put the field to noise.

Teniamocelo per noi. Sarebbe assurdo *mettere il campo a rumore* quando, fra l'altro, siamo tutt'altro che certi dell'accaduto. (Let's keep it to ourselves. It would be absurd to get everyone up in arms over it, especially since we aren't even sure of what actually took place.)

CANE (IL) Dog

Can che abbaia non morde: Barking dogs don't bite.

Cane non mangia cane: Powerful people never hurt each other.
LIT. Dog doesn't eat dog.

Drizzar le gambe ai cani: Said of futile, hopeless attempts to correct someone's ways.
LIT. To straighten dogs' legs.

Ho dovuto convincermi che tentar di cambiar quel ragazzo era voler *drizzar le gambe ai cani.* (I finally had to resign myself to the fact that I was fighting a losing battle in trying to change that boy's ways.)

Essere un cane: Said of a bad singer.
LIT. To be a dog.

Mamma mia! Hai sentito *che cani?* (Good gracious! Did you hear how they sang?)

Fa un freddo cane: It's damned cold.
LIT. It's dog cold.

Fortunato come un cane in chiesa, benvenuto come un cane in chiesa: A loser from the word go; as welcome as small-pox.

LIT. Lucky as a dog in church; welcome as a dog in church.

Era andato con un bagaglio di idee e d'entusiasmo, e l'hanno accolto *come un cane in chiesa*. (He started out full of enthusiasm and ideas and found that he was anything but welcome.)

Menare il can *per l'aia*

Menare il can per l'aia: To beat around the bush.
LIT. To lead the dog around the yard.

Non stuzzicare il can che dorme: Let sleeping dogs lie.
LIT. Do not tease a sleeping dog.

Solo come un cane: Pitifully alone.
LIT. Alone as a dog.

Tempo da cani: Horrible weather; hellish weather.
LIT. Weather for dogs.

CANNONE (IL) Cannon, gun

Essere un cannone (See also **essere un Asso**): Said of someone exceptionally skillful in a given field.
LIT. To be a cannon.

In fatto di matematica, quel ragazzo *è un cannone*. (When it comes to math, that boy is a whiz!)

CANTARE To sing

Canta che ti passa: An admonishment to take your mind off your troubles.
LIT. Sing and it will go away.

Cantar le lodi (See **Lode**)

Cantar vittoria (See **Vittoria**)

Cantarla ai sordi (See **Sordo**)

Cantarla chiara, cantarle papale papale: To spell something out; to speak one's mind; to speak up.
LIT. To sing it clear, to sing them papal papal.

Vuoi che te *la canti chiara?* In casa mia non ce lo voglio più! (Shall I spell it out for you? I don't want him in my house any more!)

Far cantare qualcuno: To get someone to talk (about confidential matters).
LIT. To make someone sing.

L'unico mezzo per *farlo cantare* è una buona mancia. (The only way to get him to talk is a good tip.)

Lasciar cantar qualcuno: To disregard someone's criticism, to let him rant and rave.
LIT. To let someone sing.

E tu *lascialo cantare!* Tanto lo sai che ha bisogno di criticar sempre tutto. (Let him talk, what do you care! Don't you know he always has to find fault with everything?)

CAPATA (**LA**) Head-push, butting

Dare una capatina: To look in on.
LIT. To give a small head-push.

Non mi sono ancora completamente rimesso, ma vado ogni giorno a *dare una capatina* in ufficio. (I'm not completely well yet, but I drop in at the office every day.)

CAPELLO (**IL**) Hair

Avere un diavolo per capello (See **Diavolo**)

Averne fin sopra i capelli: To have it up to here; to be fed up with it; to have it coming out of one's ears.
LIT. To have up to one's hair of it.

Far rizzare i capelli: To make one's hair stand on end.

Non torcere un capello a qualcuno: Not to touch a hair on someone's head.
LIT. Not to twist a hair to someone.

Spaccare un capello in quattro: To split hairs.
LIT. To split one hair in four.

Tirato per i capelli

Tirato per i capelli: Far-fetched.
LIT. Stretched by the hair.

CAPO (IL) Head (See also **Testa**)

A capofitto: Head first.

Avere il capo tra le nuvole: To have one's head in the clouds.

Aver grilli per il capo (See **Grillo**)

Capo ameno: Amusing fellow.
LIT. Jolly head.

Capo scarico: Unreliable, irresponsible person; empty-headed.
LIT. Empty head.

Cosa fatta capo ha: What's done can't be undone; the fat's in the fire.
LIT. Thing done has a head.

Dare una lavata di capo a qualcuno: To give someone a good scolding, a dressing down.
LIT. To give someone a good head washing.

Fare capolino: To peek in.
LIT. To do little head.

Grattacapo: Worry, problem, difficulty.
LIT. Head-scratcher.

Mangiar la pappa in capo a qualcuno (See **Pappa**)

Non aver né capo né coda: To make no sense.
LIT. To have neither head nor tail.

> È un ragionamento *senza capo né coda*. (It's a ridiculous argument.)

Non sapere dove battere il capo: Not to know which way to turn.
LIT. Not to know where to hit one's head.

Per sommi capi: In brief.
LIT. By main headings.

> Sarebbe troppo lungo darti tutti i dettagli. Te lo dirò *per sommi capi*. (It would take too long to go into all the details. Let me give you the gist of it.)

Tra capo e collo (See **Collo**)

CAPPELLO (IL) Hat

Prender cappello: To take offense; to get sore about something.
LIT. To take hat.

> Che gusto c'è a discutere con una persona che *prende cappello* così facilmente? (Where's the fun in arguing with someone who gets hu.t at the slightest remark?)

Attaccare il cappello al chiodo (See **Chiodo**)

Far tanto di cappello a qualcuno: To take one's hat off to someone.
LIT. To make so much of hat to someone.

Prender cappello

In fatto di musica, bisogna *fargli tanto di cappello*. (As far as knowledge of music is concerned, you really have to take your hat off to him.)

Portare il cappello sulle ventitré: To wear one's hat over one ear.
LIT. To wear one's hat on the twenty-three.

CAPRA (LA) Goat

Salvar capra e cavoli: To manage to successfully complete two seemingly incompatible undertakings.
LIT. To save the goat and the cabbages.

Sai che son poi riuscito a *salvar capra e cavoli?* Non gli ho restituito il denaro e siamo più amici di prima. (Did you know that I managed to keep both the money *and* his friendship, after all? What do you say to that?)

Capro espiatorio: Scapegoat.

CARBONE (IL) Coal

Essere sui carboni ardenti (See also **essere sulle Spine**): To be on pins and needles; on tenterhooks.
LIT. To be on burning coals.

CARICO (IL) Load, charge

Aver qualcuno a carico (See also **aver qualcuno sulle Spalle**): To have to support someone.
LIT. To have someone on load.

Persone a carico: Dependents.

Testimone a carico: Witness for the prosecution.
LIT. Witness for charge.

Va detto a suo carico che: It must be said against him that.
LIT. It must be said to his charge that.

CARITÀ (LA) Charity

Carità pelosa: Apparent generosity inspired by an ulterior motive.
LIT. Hairy charity.

No grazie! *Carità pelosa.* (No thanks! I'm sure he must have an ulterior motive.)

In camera caritatis: In confidence.
LIT. (Latin for) In charity's room.

Te lo dirò *in camera caritatis.* (I'll tell you in private.)

Per carità: For God's sake!
LIT. For charity.

CARNE (LA) Meat, flesh

Carne della propria carne: One's own flesh and blood.
LIT. Flesh of one's flesh.

Di carne ed ossa: Of flesh and blood.
LIT. Of flesh and bones.

Capirai, anch'io—dopo tutto—son fatto *di carne ed ossa.* (I'm made of flesh and blood too, you know!)

In carne ed ossa: In person; in the flesh.
LIT. In flesh and bones.

L'hai proprio visto? *In carne ed ossa?* (Did you really see him? In the flesh?)

Mettere troppa carne al fuoco: To have too many irons in the fire.
LIT. To put too much meat on the fire.

CARO Dear, expensive

Caro arrabbiato, caro appestato: Frightfully expensive.
LIT. Angry expensive, plagued expensive.

È un buon ristorante, ma non ci vado mai perché è *caro arrabbiato.* (It's a good restaurant but I never go there because it's expensive as hell.)

CARRO (IL) Cart

Essere l'ultima ruota del carro: To be the least important member of a group.
LIT. To be the last wheel of the cart.

Figurati se chiede la mia opinione. *Sono l'ultima ruota del carro!* (He wouldn't dream of asking my opinion. I'm just another cog in the wheel!)

Mettere il carro avanti ai buoi (See **Bue**)

Tirare la carretta: To go about one's everyday, dull, and painful tasks.

LIT. To pull the little cart.

> Intanto lei è in villeggiatura e io invece sempre qui a *tirare la carretta!* (She's away on vacation and I'm left here to do the dirty work.)

CARTA (**LA**) Paper, card, document

Cambiar le carte in tavola (See also **voltare la Frittata**): To change the meaning of something previously stated; or to give the wrong interpretation to someone's words.

LIT. To change the cards on the table.

> Ora *non mi cambiar le carte in tavola!* Sai bene quel che ho detto. (Now, don't twist my words. You know what I said.)

Carta canta e villan dorme: Referring to the necessity of putting agreements in writing so as to avoid later claims.

LIT. Paper sings and peasant sleeps.

Dar carta bianca a qualcuno: To give someone carte blanche, full power to act.

LIT. To give white paper to someone.

Far carte false: To go to any lengths to achieve something.

LIT. To make false documents.

> Per passare un inverno a Parigi, *farei carte false.* (I'd do anything to spend a winter in Paris.)

Fortunato in amor non giuochi a carte: Lucky at cards, unlucky in love.

LIT. Lucky in love should not play cards.

Giuocare a carte scoperte: To state one's intentions openly without holding anything back.

LIT. To play with cards uncovered, to play double dummy.

Mandare a carte quarantotto: To call the whole damned thing off.

LIT. To send to cards forty-eight.

Puntare tutto su una carta: To put all one's eggs in one basket.
LIT. To stake everything on one card.

CARTUCCIA (LA) Cartridge

L'ultima cartuccia: One's last resource.
LIT. The last cartridge.

Mezza cartuccia: A person of very limited capacities.
LIT. Half a cartridge.

CASCARE To fall

Casca e pendi: Said of a person without physical or moral energy.
LIT. Fall and lean.

Che vuoi che me ne faccia di un *cascaependi* di quel genere? (What use can I possibly have for a deadhead like him?)

Fare il cascamorto: To act love-sick; to pretend to be madly in love.
LIT. To do the fall dead.

Se crede di entrare nelle buone grazie di mio padre *facendo il cascamorto* con me, si sbaglia di grosso. (If he thinks he's going to get on the good side of my father by playing the part of the love-sick suitor, he's sadly mistaken.)

CASO (IL) Chance, case

Farci caso: To notice.
LIT. To make case at it.

Al giorno d'oggi, nessuno *ci fa più caso.* (Nowadays, nobody bats an eyelash at it.)

CASSETTA (LA) Cashbox

Far cassetta: To be good box-office material.
LIT. To make cashbox.

Film di cassetta, lavoro di cassetta: Financial success.
LIT. Cashbox motion picture, cashbox work.

CATINELLA (**LA**) Bucket, basin

Piovere a catinelle: To come down (to rain) in buckets, cats and dogs.

CATTEDRA (**LA**) Professorial chair

Montare in cattedra: To assume a pompous and condescending manner; to pontificate.
LIT. To climb on the professorial chair.

CAVALLO (**IL**) Horse

A caval donato non si guarda in bocca: Don't look a gift horse in the mouth!

Campa cavallo ché l'erba cresce: Don't hold your breath!
LIT. Go on living, horse, for the grass is growing.

Ha detto che quest'anno non può permettersi aumenti di stipendio. Se le cose andranno bene, forse l'anno prossimo . . . Sì, *campa cavallo!* (He said he can't afford to give salary increases this year. If business is good maybe next year . . . but don't hang by your thumbs!)

Cavallo di battaglia: An artist's forte, pièce de résistance, old stand-by.
LIT. War horse.

Correre la cavallina: To sow one's wild oats.
LIT. To run the little mare.

Essere a cavallo

Essere a cavallo: To have won half the battle; to be well on the way.
LIT. To be on horseback.

L'occhio del padrone ingrassa il cavallo (See **Occhio**)

Montare sul caval d'Orlando: To get up on one's high horse.
LIT. To climb on Orlando's horse.

CAVOLO (IL) Cabbage

Andare a piantar cavoli: To retire from active life.
LIT. To go to plant cabbages.

> Un anno tutt'al più e me ne *vado a piantar cavoli.* (Another year at the most, and I'm going to go on a permanent vacation.)

Cavoli riscaldati: Said of attempts to revive old ideas, endeavors, or relationships.
LIT. Reheated cabbage.

> È inutile che cerchiate di farmelo incontrare. Non sarebbero che *cavoli riscaldati.* (Please don't try to arrange a meeting between us. It's all over and done with.)

Come i cavoli a merenda: Utterly and absolutely out of place.
LIT. Like cabbages at afternoon tea.

Non me ne importa un cavolo (See also **non me ne importa un Corno, un Fico**): I don't care a rap; I don't give a hoot.
LIT. It doesn't matter a cabbage to me.

Salvare capra e cavoli (See **Capra**)

CENTESIMO (IL) Penny

Guardare al centesimo: To pinch pennies.
LIT. To look at the penny.

CERVELLO (IL) Brain

Avere un cervello d'oca (See **Oca**)

Bruciarsi le cervella: To blow one's brains out.
LIT. To burn one's brains.

Dar di volta il cervello: To go mad.
LIT. To have the brain turn over.

> Ti ha forse *dato di volta il cervello?* (What's the matter? Have you gone nuts, or something?)

Lambiccarsi il cervello: To rack one's brains.
LIT. To distill one's brain.

CHIARO Clear

Dire chiaro e tondo: To say *exactly* what one thinks; to make no bones about something.
LIT. To say clear and round.

CHILO (IL) Chyle

Fare il chilo: To rest after meals.
LIT. To make the chyle.

> Possibile che alla tua età tu non possa fare a meno del *chilo* dopo mangiato? (You're not that old, do you really have to lie down after dinner?)

CHINA (LA) Slope

Essere su una brutta china: To be on a morally dangerous path.
LIT. To be on an ugly slope.

Lasciar correr l'acqua per la sua china (See **Acqua**)

CHIODO (IL) Nail

Attaccare il cappello al chiodo: To settle down, especially in a wealthy marriage.
LIT. To hang the hat on the nail.

Avere un chiodo fisso: To be constantly driven by a single preoccupation.
LIT. To have a fixed nail.

> *Ha il chiodo fisso* della figlia e non si è mai goduta una vacanza in vita sua. (She's so obsessed with worry about her daughter that she hasn't enjoyed a single vacation in her entire life.)

Chiodo scaccia chiodo: One evil gets rid of another.
LIT. Nail drives out nail.

Attaccare il cappello al chiodo

Esser pieno di chiodi: To have a great many debts.
LIT. To be full of nails.

Magro come un chiodo: Thin as a rail.
LIT. Thin as a nail.

Non batter un chiodo: To accomplish nothing.
LIT. Not to hit one nail.

> Sì, la laurea due anni fa l'ha presa, ma m'hanno detto che *non batte un chiodo*. (Yes, he did graduate two years ago, but I hear he hasn't done a thing since.)

Piantar chiodi: To incur debts.
LIT. To plant nails.

Roba da chiodi (See also **roba da Pazzi**): You don't say! Unbelievable! It's unheard of!
LIT. Stuff worthy of nails.

Stare al chiodo: To keep one's nose to the grindstone.
LIT. To stay at the nail.

CIECO Blind

In terra di ciechi, beato chi ha un occhio: In the country of the blind the one-eyed man is king.
LIT. In the country of the blind, happy he who has an eye.

/ 47

Mosca cieca (See **Mosca**)

Non aver più un soldo da far cantare un cieco: Not to have a red cent.
LIT. Not to have a penny left to make a blind man sing.

Vicolo cieco: Blind alley.

CIELO (IL) Sky, heaven

Apriti cielo: All hell breaks loose!
LIT. Open up heaven.

> È bello buono e caro, ma basta arrivare mezz'ora più tardi in ufficio . . . *apriti cielo!* (He's as sweet as can be, but just try coming in half an hour late and there's hell to pay!)

Attaccarsi alle funi in cielo: To go to any lengths to prove a point.
LIT. To cling to the ropes in the sky.

Essere al settimo cielo: To be in seventh heaven.

Fulmine a ciel sereno: Bolt out of the blue.
LIT. Lightning in a clear sky.

Non stare né in cielo né in terra: To be utter nonsense.
LIT. Not to be either in heaven or on earth.

> Scusami, ma il tuo modo di ragionare *non sta né in cielo né in terra.* (I'm sorry, but you're talking through your hat.)

Portare qualcuno ai sette cieli: To praise someone to the skies.
LIT. To bring someone to the seven heavens.

Smuovere cielo e terra: To move heaven and earth; to leave no stone unturned.

Toccare il cielo con un dito: To be on top of the world; to be walking on air.

LIT. To touch the sky with a finger.

CIMA (LA) Peak

Non essere una cima: To be no genius.
LIT. Not to be a peak.

CINTOLA (LA) Belt, waist

Star con le mani alla cintola (See also **star con le mani in Mano, star con le mani in Tasca**): To be idle, passive; to stand by with one's hands in one's pockets; to twiddle one's thumbs.
LIT. To stay with one's hands in one's belt.

CINTURA (LA) Belt

Stringersi la cintura: To pull in one's belt; to tighten one's belt another notch.

CODA (LA) Tail

Andarsene con la coda fra le gambe: To leave with one's tail between one's legs.

Aver la coda di paglia (See **Paglia**)

Attaccarsi alle funi in cielo

Fare la coda, mettersi in coda: To stand in line, to line up.
LIT. To make the tail; to put oneself in tail.

Guardare con la coda dell'occhio: To watch out of the corner of one's eye.
LIT. To look with the tail of one's eye.

Quando il diavolo ci mette la coda (See **Diavolo**)

Saper dove il diavolo tiene la coda (See **Diavolo**)

COLLERA (LA) Rage, anger

Montare in collera: To fly into a rage.
LIT. To climb in rage.

COLLO (IL) Neck

Andare a rotta di collo (See also **andare a Rotoli**): To deteriorate; to go to the dogs.
LIT. To go at breakneck speed.

> Purtroppo, i suoi affari *stanno andando a rotta di collo.* (Unfortunately, his business is rapidly going downhill.)

A rotta di collo: At breakneck speed.

Fare allungare il collo a qualcuno: To keep someone waiting a long time.
LIT. To make someone's neck grow longer.

Farsi mettere i piedi sul collo (See **Piede**)

Lasciare le briglie sul collo: To give free rein.
LIT. To leave the reins on the neck.

Prendere qualcuno per il collo: To take advantage of someone.
LIT. To take someone by the neck.

Rimetterci l'osso del collo: To come out of a situation very badly.
LIT. To lose the bone of one's neck.

> È una pagina chiusa, ma *ci ho rimesso l'osso del collo.* (It's all over now, but I lost my shirt in the process.)

Saltare al collo di qualcuno: To throw one's arms around someone's neck.
LIT. To jump on someone's neck.

Tra capo e collo: Unexpectedly and at a not very convenient time.

LIT. Between head and neck.

Ero pronto a partire, quando mi è arrivato *tra capo e collo* un lavoro urgente. (I was all ready to leave, when a rush job came in and there I was—stuck!)

COLMO (IL) Peak, top

Questo è il colmo: That's the limit! That tops them all! LIT. This is the peak.

COLORE (IL) Color

Diventare di tutti i colori: To show deep embarrassment; to turn a hundred shades of red. LIT. To turn all colors.

Farne, dirne, vederne di tutti i colori: To do, say, or see all kinds of wild, preposterous things. LIT. To do, say, see, things of all colors.

COLPO (IL) Blow

A colpo sicuro: With no risks involved. LIT. At sure hit.

Se scegli un giovedì, ci vai *a colpo sicuro* perché quel giorno è sempre in ufficio. (If you pick a Thursday, you can't go wrong because he's always there that day.)

Colpo di grazia: The crowning blow; the coup de grâce; the last straw.

Ero già stanco morto. Quell'invito a cena mi ha dato *il colpo di grazia.* (I was already dead tired, but that dinner date really finished me.)

Colpo di scena: Unexpected dramatic move, sudden and striking development. LIT. Stage coup.

Hai saputo del *colpo di scena* nell'affare X? (Have you heard the latest in the X affair? Isn't it amazing?)

Colpo di telefono: Telephone call.
LIT. Telephone blow.

Vuoi che ti dia *un colpo di telefono* stasera per confermare? (Shall I give you a ring tonight and confirm it?)

Far colpo: To make a hit, a big impression.

COMPLIMENTO (IL) Compliment

Fare complimenti: To stand on ceremony; to be afraid to impose.
LIT. To do compliments.

Ora che sua moglie è in villeggiatura, *non faccia complimenti* e venga a cena da noi ogni volta che crede. (Now that your wife is away for the summer, please feel free to come over for dinner any time.)

Fare un complimento: To pay a compliment.
LIT. To make a compliment.

CONTENTO Happy, satisfied

Contento come una Pasqua: Happy as a lark; as pleased as Punch.
LIT. Happy as an Easter.

Contento lui, contenti tutti: As long as he's happy . . .
LIT. Happy he, happy everyone.

Fare qualcuno contento e canzonato: To grant someone's request with a token gesture.
LIT. To make someone satisfied and made fun of.

Non capisci che questo pezzo di carta non li lega in nessun modo? *T'hanno fatto contento e canzonato!* (Don't you understand that this piece of paper doesn't bind them in any way? They've made a fool of you!)

CONTO (IL) Account, calculation, check

A conti fatti: Everything considered.
LIT. At accounts made.

Fare i conti addosso a qualcuno, fare i conti in tasca a qualcuno: To pry into someone's financial affairs.
LIT. To balance the books on someone; to balance the books in someone's pocket.

Dio sa che non mi piace *fare i conti addosso a nessuno*, ma dubito che col suo stipendio possa permettersi un viaggio come questo. (God knows I don't like to stick my nose into other people's business, but I doubt he can afford a trip like this on his salary.)

Fare i conti con qualcuno: To take care of someone; to settle things with him once and for all.
LIT. To balance the books with someone.

Quanto a X, puoi dirgli che *farò i conti con lui* alla prima occasione. (As for X, you can tell him that I'll settle with him the first chance I get.)

Fare i conti senza l'oste (See **Oste**)

Resa dei conti: Day of reckoning.
LIT. Presentation of financial statements.

CONTRARIO Contrary

Fare il Bastian contrario: To say "no" out of habit or temperament, rather than on the basis of considered opinion; "Contrary Joe."
LIT. To do the contrary Sebastian.

CORAGGIO (IL) Courage

Coraggio: Chin up! Step on it! Let's get going!

Prendere il coraggio a due mani: To take one's courage in both hands.

CORDA (LA) Rope, string

Aver più di una corda al proprio arco: To have two strings to one's bow.
LIT. To have more than one string to one's bow.

Dar corda (See also **dar Spago**): To lead someone on, to encourage someone to talk.
LIT. To give rope.

Essere alle corde: To be on the ropes.

Essere giù di corda: To be tired; to be down in the dumps; to be under the weather.
LIT. To be down of rope.

Mostrar la corda: Said of something that is worn out.
LIT. To show the rope.

Ha un certo spirito, anche se alcune delle sue barzellette *mostrano un po' la corda.* (He's got a sense of humor, although some of his jokes are a bit dated.)

Parlare di corda in casa dell'impiccato: To bring up a touchy subject; to talk of hemp in the house of the hanged.

Tagliare la corda: To sneak out.
LIT. To cut the rope.

Tagliare la corda

Tirare la corda: To go too far.
LIT. To pull the rope.

Non mi meraviglio che abbia finito per arrabbiarsi. Hai

veramente *tirato troppo la corda.* (I'm not surprised she finally hit the roof. You really pushed things too far.)

CORNO (IL) Horn

Non me ne importa un corno (See also **non me ne importa un Cavolo, un Fico**): I don't care a rap; I don't give a hoot.
LIT. It doesn't matter a horn to me.

Prendere il toro per le corna (See **Toro**)

CORPO (IL) Body

A corpo morto: With great energy; to the point of exhaustion.
LIT. At dead body.

COSCIENZA (LA) Conscience

Avere la coscienza pulita: To have a clear conscience.
LIT. To have a clean conscience.

Avere la coscienza sporca: To have a guilty conscience.
LIT. To have a dirty conscience.

Per scrupolo di coscienza: Just to put one's mind at rest.
LIT. Out of scruple of conscience.

So che tu non badi a queste cose, ma *per scrupolo di coscienza* voglio dirti che in campagna non abbiamo ancora la luce elettrica. (I know you won't mind, but I feel it's only fair to tell you that up in the country we still don't have electricity.)

COTTO Cooked, baked

Dirne di cotte e di crude a qualcuno: To give someone a piece of one's mind; to rake someone over the coals.
LIT. To say cooked ones and raw ones to someone.

Essere innamorato cotto: To be head over heels in love.
LIT. To be cooked in love.

Furbo di tre cotte: A smart operator.
LIT. A shrewd one of three bakings.

Prendere una cotta, avere una cotta: To get a crush on someone; to have a crush on someone.
LIT. To take a baking; to have a baking.

CRESTA (LA) Rooster's comb, ridge, crest

Abbassare la cresta: To draw in one's horns.
LIT. To lower the comb.

Alzare la cresta: To get cocky.
LIT. To raise one's comb.

Fare la cresta: To pad the bills (usually used in connection with housekeepers and the shopping that is entrusted to them).
LIT. To make the crest.

CROCE (LA) Cross

A occhio e croce: Roughly; offhand; approximately.
LIT. By eye and cross.

Dare la croce addosso a qualcuno: To persistently speak of someone in a disparaging manner; to harass, torment him.
LIT. To hit someone with the cross.

> Perché *gli dai sempre la croce addosso?* È tutt'altro che un cattivo ragazzo. (Why are you always picking on him? He's not a bad guy.)

Fare a testa e croce (See **Testa**)

Farci una croce sopra: To give something up once and for all; to call it quits.
LIT. To make a cross over it.

CUCCHIAIO (IL) Spoon

Essere da raccogliersi col cucchiaino: To be exhausted.
LIT. To be (in such a condition) to be picked up with a teaspoon.

Dopo una settimana di quella vita, *ero da raccogliersi col cucchiaino.* (After a week of that kind of life, I was ready for the hospital.)

CUCCO (IL) Cuckoo

Vecchio come il cucco: As old as the hills.
LIT. Old as the cuckoo.

CUCINARE To cook

Cucinare qualcuno a dovere: To handle someone the way he deserves; to cook his goose.
LIT. To cook someone the right way.

CUFFIA (LA) Bonnet

Per il rotto della cuffia: By the skin of one's teeth.
LIT. By the tear of the bonnet.

CUOIO (IL) Hide, leather

Tirare le cuoia: To die; to kick the bucket.
LIT. To draw one's hides.

CUORE (IL) Heart

Avere il cuore in gola: To have one's heart in one's mouth.

Cuor contento: Said of an even-tempered, contented person.
LIT. Happy heart.

Ha una faccia da *cuor contento.* (He looks like such an easygoing person.)

Mettersi una mano sul cuore: To speak one's mind in all honesty.
LIT. To put one's hand on one's heart.

Mettiti una mano sul cuore e dimmi se non ho sempre agito per il tuo meglio. (Think about it, and tell me in all honesty if I haven't had your interests at heart all along.)

Parlare a cuore aperto: To speak frankly, open-heartedly.
LIT. To speak with open heart.

Parlare a qualcuno con il cuore in mano: To speak to someone in all sincerity; from the bottom of one's heart.
LIT. To talk to someone with one's heart in one's hand.

Stare a cuore a qualcuno: To matter a great deal.
LIT. To be at heart to someone.

Mi raccomando, occupati di quella faccenda! Ricordati che *mi sta molto a cuore*. (Please remember to take care of that matter. It really means a lot to me!)

D

DANNO (IL) Damage

Aggiungere al danno le beffe: To add insult to injury.
LIT. To add to the damage the mockery.

DARE To give

A chi ne dà e a chi ne promette: Said of an impossible, antagonistic person.
LIT. Some he beats up, and to some he promises beatings.

> Davvero non ci si ragiona più. *A chi ne dà e a chi ne promette.* (He's really become impossible! He finds fault with everything!)

Dai, picchia e mena; dagli oggi, dagli domani
LIT. Give, knock, and beat up; give it to him today, give it to him tomorrow.

Come sono riuscito a farlo studiare per gli esami? Che vuoi, *dai, picchia e mena,* s'è convinto anche lui. (How did I get him to study for his exams? Sheer nagging, my dear!)

Dare del lei, dare del tu: To address someone with the formal or familiar form.
LIT. To give of the "lei," to give of the "tu."

Dare dello stupido, del ladro, ecc.: To call someone a dumbbell, a thief, etc.
LIT. To give of the stupid, of the thief, etc.

DEBOLE (IL) Weakness

Avere un debole per: To have a weakness for something; to have a soft spot for someone.

DENARO (IL) Money

Denaro e santità metà della metà: All statements regarding both money and saintliness should be taken with a grain of salt.
LIT. Money and holiness, half of half.

Far denaro a palate: To make money hand over fist.
LIT. To make money by shovelfuls.

DENTE (IL) Tooth

A denti stretti: In a threatening voice.
LIT. At clenched teeth.

Al dente: Slightly undercooked.
LIT. To the tooth.

Avere il dente avvelenato contro qualcuno: To be dead set against someone; to have it in for someone.
LIT. To have the poisoned tooth against someone.

Tutti sanno che *hai il dente avvelenato contro* quel poveraccio. (Everyone knows you have it in for that poor guy.)

Legare i denti, allegare i denti: To set one's teeth on edge.
LIT. To bind one's teeth; to alloy one's teeth.

Mostrare i denti: To show one's teeth.

Non toccare un dente: Not to satisfy one's hunger in the least.

LIT. Not to touch one tooth.

Quello spuntino *non mi ha toccato un dente.* Ho più fame di prima! (That snack didn't do a thing for me. I'm just as hungry as I was before!)

Regger l'anima coi denti (See **Anima**)

DIAVOLO (IL) Devil

Abitare a casa del diavolo: To live in a remote, Godforsaken part of town.

LIT. To live at the devil's home.

Andare al diavolo, andare all'inferno: To go to the devil, to hell.

Avere il diavolo in corpo: To be full of the devil.

LIT. To have the devil in one's body.

Avere un diavolo per capello: To be extremely irritated; to be in a hell of a bad mood.

LIT. To have a devil for each hair.

Ti consiglio di non entrare nel suo ufficio stamani. *Ha un diavolo per capello.* (Take my advice and stay out of his office this morning. He sure looks mad at the world.)

Avere un diavolo *per capello*

Buon diavolo (See also **buona Pasta**): Good egg.
LIT. Good devil.

Chi dà e poi toglie il diavolo se lo raccoglie: A threat to Indian givers.
LIT. Who gives and then takes back, the devil gets hold of him.

Essere come il diavolo e l'acqua santa: To be incompatible; to mix like oil and water.
LIT. To be like the devil and holy water.

Fare il diavolo a quattro: To do everything in one's power; to make lots of noise, to raise hell.
LIT. To do the devil by four.

> *Ha fatto il diavolo a quattro* per farsi trasferire, ma non c'è riuscito. (He did everything under the sun to get a transfer, but he didn't succeed.)

Far l'avvocato del diavolo, far la parte del diavolo (See **Avvocato**)

Il diavolo insegna a far la pentola, ma non il coperchio: Murder will out.
LIT. The devil teaches how to make the pot, but not the cover.

Il diavolo non è sempre brutto come si dipinge: Things are not always as bad as they seem.
LIT. The devil isn't always as ugly as he is painted.

La farina del diavolo va tutta in crusca: Nothing good ever comes from ill-gotten gains.
LIT. The devil's flour becomes all bran.

Mandare qualcuno o qualcosa al diavolo: To send someone packing; to call something off in anger.
LIT. To send someone or something to the devil.

Quando il diavolo ci mette la coda
LIT. When the devil puts his tail in it.

> È inutile, *quando il diavolo ci mette la coda* . . . è meglio non pensarci più. (I tell you this thing was jinxed from the start . . . we might as well forget it.)

Sapere dove il diavolo tiene la coda: To know a thing or two.
LIT. To know where the devil keeps his tail.

Saperne una più del diavolo: To go the devil one better, to outsmart the devil; to be extremely smart and resourceful.
LIT. To know one more of them than the devil.

> Non mi meraviglio che se la sia cavata da una situazione così difficile. Quello *ne sa una più del diavolo*. (I'm not at all surprised that he managed to get out of that mess. That guy knows every trick in the book.)

DIFENDERE To defend

Difendersi: To perform adequately (said in a light vein); to hold one's own.
LIT. To defend oneself.

> Giuochi bene a tennis? Grazie, *mi difendo!* ("Are you a good tennis player?" "I get by, thank you!")

DIO God

A chi non ha da far Dio glielo manda: A playful reference to the fact that busy people seem to attract new work and responsibilities.
LIT. To him who has nothing to do God sends it.

Dagli amici mi guardi Iddio, ché dai nemici mi guardo io (See **Amico**)

Deus ex machina*: Skillful and powerful person, who comes in to solve an intricate situation.
LIT. (Latin for) God from the machinery.

Dio ce la mandi buona: God help us!
LIT. May God sent it to us good.

Dio ce ne scampi e liberi: God forbid!
LIT. May God save us and free us from it.

Dio li fa e poi li appaia: Birds of a feather flock together.
LIT. God makes them and then joins (matches) them.

---

* Reference to the sudden and eventful appearance in ancient theatrical performances of gods assisted by some kind of contraption.

Dio manda il freddo secondo i panni: God tempers the wind to the shorn lamb.
LIT. God doesn't pay only on Saturday (payday).

Dio non paga il sabato: An admonition to behave well, for the day of reckoning may come at any time.
LIT. God doesn't pay only on Saturday (payday).

È quel che Dio comanda: It's just what the doctor ordered.
LIT. It's what God orders.

Essere fuori dalla grazia di Dio: To be raving mad.
LIT. To be out of the grace of God.

> Hai fatto bene a non venire; *era proprio fuori dalla grazia di Dio!* (It's a good thing you didn't come today. He was absolutely furious at you.)

Render l'anima a Dio: To give up the ghost.
LIT. To give back one's soul to God.

Vien giù l'ira di Dio: Said of an exceptionally heavy rainstorm.
LIT. The wrath of God is coming down.

DIRE To say

A dir molto: And that's saying a lot.
LIT. To say a great deal.

Ci vuol più a dirlo che a farlo: It's more trouble to talk about it than to actually do it.
LIT. It needs more to say it than to do it.

> Vieni, ti aiuto io. Ti assicuro che *ci vuol più a dirlo che a farlo.* (Come on, I'll help you. I assure you that it looks harder than it really is.)

Dei suoi se ne vuol dire, ma non se ne vuol sentire: One wants to criticize one's own but not to hear them criticized.

Dire la sua: To put in one's two-cents' worth.
LIT. To say one's own.

Dirle grosse (See **Grosso**)

Dirne due a qualcuno, dirne quattro a qualcuno: To tell someone a thing or two; to give someone a piece of one's mind.

LIT. To tell two of them to someone, to tell four of them to someone.

Senza dire né ai né bai: Without so much as a how-do-you-do.
LIT. Without saying either "ai" or "bai."

Sia detto fra noi: Just between us; between you and me and the lamppost.
LIT. Let it be said between us.

DITO (IL) Finger

Avere il dito verde: To have a green thumb.
LIT. To have the green finger.

Avere qualcosa sulle punta delle dita: To have something at one's fingertips.

Conoscere qualcosa a menadito: To know something inside out.
LIT. To know something to "menadito" (used only in this expression).

Leccarsi le dita (See also **leccarsi i Baffi, le Labbra**): To lick one's chops.
LIT. To lick one's fingers.

Legarsela al dito: To remember a wrong bitterly.
LIT. To bind it to one's finger.

Questa poi è imperdonabile e *me la lego al dito*. (This is really unforgivable and I'll always hold it against him.)

Mettere il dito sulla piaga (See **Piaga**)

Mordersi le dita (See also **mordersi le Mani**): To feel like kicking oneself for something done.

Legarsela al dito

LIT. To bite one's fingers.

Mostrare a dito: To single out.
LIT. To show with finger.

Tra moglie e marito non mettere il dito: Advice against interfering in conjugal matters.
LIT. Between wife and husband do not put your finger.

DONNA (LA) Woman

Chi dice donna dice danno: Women are synonymous with damage.
LIT. Who says woman says damage.

Donna allegra: Loose woman; woman of easy virtue.
LIT. Merry woman.

Donna di facili costumi: Woman of easy morals.

Donna specchiante poco filante: Vain women are not good workers.
LIT. Woman at the mirror spins little.

Figlio di una buona donna: Son of a ———.
LIT. Son of a good woman.

Nè donna nè tela a lume di candela: Neither women nor linen (should be chosen) by candlelight.

Quel che donna vuole Dio lo vuole: It is of little use to try to oppose a woman's will.
LIT. What woman wants God wants.

DORMIRE To sleep

Dormire come un ghiro: To sleep like a log.
LIT. To sleep like a dormouse.

Dormire della grossa: To sleep like a log, to be a sound sleeper.
LIT. To sleep of the big.

Dormire fra due guanciali: To rest easy; to be completely relaxed about a situation; to have complete trust in someone. LIT. To sleep between two pillows.

Se hai affidato la causa all'avvocato X, puoi *dormire fra due guanciali.* È un uomo meraviglioso! (If you turned the case over to X, you don't have to give it another thought. He's great!)

DOZZINA (LA) Dozen, room and board

Da dozzina: Cheap; commonplace; worthless.
LIT. For dozen.

Prendere a dozzina: To take boarders.
LIT. To take at room and board.

Dormire *fra due guanciali*

Stare a dozzina da qualcuno: To board with someone.
LIT. To be at room and board at someone's house.

DUNQUE Then

Venire al dunque: To come to the point; when it comes right down to it.
LIT. To come to the then.

Dice sempre che vorrebbe aiutarci, ma quando *si viene al dunque . . .* (He's always saying he'd love to help us out, but when the time comes . . .)

E

EGITTO Egypt

Che———d'Egitto!

LIT. What———of Egypt.

Ma *che caldo d'Egitto!* È una giornata ideale per una gita in barca. (Too hot? You're nuts! It's a perfect day for sailing.) *Che amicizia d'Egitto!* Queste son cose che non si possono perdonare. (Friendship my eye! This kind of behavior is unforgivable.)

ENTRARE To enter

Questo non c'entra: That's beside the point!

LIT. This does not enter into it.

EPOCA (L') Epoch

Fare epoca: To make history.

LIT. To make epoch.

Si figuri se non mi ricordo di Lei. I suoi racconti di quella sera *fecero epoca!* (As if I could have forgotten you! The stories you told that night went down in history!)

ERBA (L') Grass

Dare l'erba cassia: To give someone the air, the axe.
LIT. To give someone the "Cassia" grass.

Fare d'ogni erba un fascio: To lump good and bad together; to behave without discrimination out of anger or haste.
LIT. To make one bundle of all (types of) grass.

Ma si tratta di due casi completamente diversi. *Tu fai d'ogni erbà un fascio.* (But we're talking about two completely different things. You can't generalize that way.)

In erba: Not in full bloom, yet showing good promise.
LIT. In grass.

Guarda come ci sa fare! Un vero dottore *in erba!* (See how he goes about it. A budding doctor!)

Mangiarsi il grano in erba: To dispose of one's earnings in advance.
LIT. To eat one's wheat in grass.

A *mangiarsi il grano in erba,* come fai tu, si finisce sulla paglia. (If you spend your money before you have it, you'll end up broke.)

Pascere qualcuno d'erba trastulla: To encourage someone's hopes or expectations with unrealistic promises.
LIT. To feed someone with play grass.

Non sono tipo da *pascere un amico d'erba trastulla,* e preferisco dirti fin d'ora di non farci assegnamento. (I'm not the type to lead on a friend, and I'd rather tell you right now not to count on it.)

Sentir nascer l'erba: To have very sharp hearing.
LIT. To hear the grass grow.

ESTATE (L') Summer

Estate di San Martino: Indian summer.
LIT. St. Martin's (Nov. 11) summer.

F

FACCIA (LA) Face

Faccia di bronzo: Brazen-faced person.
LIT. Face of bronze.

Faccia tosta: Nerve; cheek; gall.
LIT. Hard face.

Ci vuole *una bella faccia tosta* per parlare in questo modo! (It takes some nerve to talk that way!) Che razza di *faccia tosta!* (Of all the unmitigated gall!)

Salvare la faccia: To save face.

Viva la faccia: More power to him! Good for him! Hats off to him!
LIT. Long live the face.

Gli hai detto come la pensavi? *Viva la faccia!* (You told

him what you thought? Good for you!) *Viva la faccia di*
X, che è sempre pronto a darti una mano. (Hats off to X
who's always ready to give you a hand.)

FARE To do, to make

Abbiamo fatto trenta, facciamo trentuno: We've gone this
far, let's finish the job.
LIT. We have made thirty, let's make thirty-one.

Chi non fa non falla: Said to encourage, rather than dis-
courage, action.
LIT. He who doesn't act doesn't err.

Fa proprio per me: It's just my cup of tea.
LIT. It just does for me.

Fare come pare e piace: To do exactly as one pleases.
LIT. To do as it seems and pleases.

Fare fagotto: To pack up and go.
LIT. To make bundle.

Quando mi son reso conto della situazione, l'ho pregato di
far fagotto e di non rimettere mai più piede in casa mia.
(When I realized what was going on, I told him to get out
and stay out.)

Far faville: To succeed brilliantly; to scintillate.
LIT. To make sparks.

Non riconosceresti la vecchia ditta. L'ha presa in mano X
e *fa faville*. (You wouldn't know it was the same company.
X took over and he's doing wonders.)

Far fuori qualcuno (See **Fuori**)

Far furore: To be the rage.
LIT. To make furor.

Fare l'articolo: To emphasize the good qualities of something or someone; to give a sales talk.
LIT. To make the article.

Lo conosco da anni, sai. Non ho bisogno che tu *me ne*

faccia l'articolo. (I've known him for years, you know. You don't have to waste any breath telling me how good he is.)

Fare la fame: To live from hand to mouth.
LIT. To do the hunger.

Fare le cose alla Carlona: To do things sloppily.
LIT. To do things the Carlona way.

Ti prego, fallo con cura, non *alla Carlona* com'è il tuo solito. (Please do it carefully. Don't botch it up the way you usually do.)

Fare lo gnorri, fare il nesci: To feign ignorance, to play dumb.
LIT. To do the "gnorri," to do the "nesci" (used only in this context).

Andiamo, via, non *fare lo gnorri!* (Come on now, don't act so innocent!)

Fare orecchi da mercante (See also **fare l'indiano**): To turn a deaf ear.
LIT. To make merchant's ears.

Fare un casus belli di qualcosa, fare un affare di stato di qualcosa: To make a Federal case out of something.
LIT. To make a case for war, an affair of state out of something.

Farla finita: To cut it out, to stop it.
LIT. To make it finished.

Falla finita! (Cut it out!)

Farne delle sue: To be up to one's old tricks.
LIT. To do of one's own.

Farne più di Carlo in Francia: To lead an extraordinarily exciting life.
LIT. To do more of them than Charlemagne in France.

Quello è un tipo che deve *averne fatte più di Carlo in Francia.* (He's the type who must have led quite a life!)

FATTO (IL) Fact, deed

Dire il fatto suo a qualcuno: To tell someone off; to give someone a piece of one's mind.
LIT. To say his fact to someone.

Fatti maschi parole femmine: A play on the different gender of the two words, "deeds" and "words," suggesting that women talk and men act.
LIT. Deeds men words women.

Ipso facto: Immediately.
LIT. (Latin for) In the same fact.

> Non solo l'ha offerto, ma *ipso facto* è andato a casa a prenderlo. (Not only did he offer—he went home to get it right then and there.)

Sapere il fatto proprio: To know one's business, one's way around.
LIT. To know one's own fact.

> Dì quel che ti pare, ma quello è un uomo che *sa il fatto suo*. (Say what you like about him, there's a man who knows what he's talking about.)

FEGATO (IL) Liver

Aver fegato: To have guts.
LIT. To have liver.

Farsi cattivo fegato (See also **farsi cattivo Sangue**): To worry a great deal and bitterly over something.
LIT. To make oneself bad liver.

Mangiarsi il fegato: To eat one's heart out.
LIT. To eat one's liver.

FERRO (IL) Iron

Battere il ferro finché è caldo (See **Battere**)

Essere ai ferri corti: To be at swords' points, at loggerheads.
LIT. To be at short irons.

Mi hanno detto che tu ed X *siete proprio ai ferri corti.*
È vero? (Is it true that you and X are on very bad terms?)

Salute di ferro: Iron constitution.
LIT. Health of iron.

Tocca ferro: Knock on wood!
LIT. Touch iron.

FESTA (LA) Celebration, party, holiday, patron saint's day

Conciar qualcuno per le feste: To give someone a good beating.
LIT. To dress someone for the party.

Far festa: To stay home from work; to take the day off.
LIT. To make holiday.

Far festa a qualcuno: To greet someone warmly.
LIT. To make holiday to someone.

Far la festa a qualcuno: To do someone in.
LIT. To make the holiday to someone.

Per celebrare l'avvenimento, *abbiamo fatto la festa a* un paio di magnifici polli. (To celebrate, we roasted a couple of wonderful chickens.)

Guastafeste: Party-pooper; wet blanket; kill-joy.
LIT. Spoiler of parties.

Passata la festa gabbato lo santo: Once on shore we pray no more.
LIT. Passed the holiday, the saint is deceived.

Sì, aveva detto che avrebbe tenuto la macchina sempre a mia disposizione, ma ora che gliel'abbiamo comprata, capirai, *passata la festa* . . . (She did say she'd be willing to chauffeur me around, but now that we've actually bought her a car it's a different story . . .)

FIASCO (IL) Flask

Essere un fiasco: To be a flop.
LIT. To be a flask.

Far fiasco: To fail.
LIT. To make a flask.

Prendere fischi per fiaschi (See also **prendere Lucciole per lanterne**): To mistake one thing for another, not to know chalk from cheese.
LIT. To mistake whistles for flasks.

> Mi sembra impossibile. Sei sicuro che non *hai preso fischi per fiaschi?* (I can't believe it. Are you sure you weren't just seeing things?)

FIATO (IL) Breath

Col fiato sospeso: With bated breath.
LIT. With breath suspended.

Correre a perdifiato: To run as fast as one can.
LIT. To run at losing breath.

Gridare a perdifiato: To scream relentlessly.
LIT. To scream at losing breath.

> *Ho gridato a perdifiato* ma nessuno mi ha sentito. (I shouted myself hoarse, but nobody heard me.)

FICO (IL) Fig

Far le nozze coi fichi secchi (See **Nozze**)

Non me ne importa un fico (See also **non me ne importa un Cavolo, un Corno**): I don't care a rap; I don't give a hoot.
LIT. It doesn't matter a fig to me.

Serbar la pancia per i fichi: To be a coward; to be constantly afraid of getting into trouble.
LIT. To keep one's stomach for the figs.

FIGLIO (IL) Son

A chi figlio a chi figliastro (See also **usare due Pesi e due misure**): To use a double standard (said teasingly).
LIT. To some son and to some stepson.

> Vergogna! *A chi figlio e a chi figliastro,* eh? (Shame on you! What did I do to deserve the Cinderella treatment?)

Essere tutto figlio del proprio padre: To be a chip off the old block.
LIT. To be one's father's son.

Figlio di papà: Spoiled, pampered young man.
LIT. Daddy's son.

FIGURA (LA) Figure

Fare una brutta figura, fare una figuraccia, fare una figura barbina: To make a bad impression; to make a fool of oneself.
LIT. To make a bad figure.

Che brutta figura! (What a fool he made of himself!)

Fare un figurone: To make a beautiful impression; to come through with flying colors.
LIT. To make a big figure.

Devo ringraziarti, ché ieri sera col tuo vestito da sera *ho fatto un figurone.* (I'll be forever grateful to you. I really made a hit last night in your evening dress.)

FILARE To spin

Filare: Said of two people carrying on a flirtation, going together.

Non ti sei accorto che *filano da parecchi mesi?* (Hadn't you noticed that they've been going together for quite a while?)

Filare: To leave; to go under pressure; to scram.

T'ho detto di *filare.* (I told you to get going!)

Filare all'inglese: To leave unnoticed, to take French leave.
LIT. To leave the English way.

Filare *all'inglese*

Non è più il tempo che Berta filava: Times have changed.
LIT. This is no longer the time when (Queen) Bertha used to work at the spinning wheel.

FILO (IL) Thread

Bugia cucita di fil bianco: An awkward, obvious lie.
LIT. A lie sewn with white thread.

Dare del filo da torcere: To be difficult to handle.
LIT. To give thread to twist.

Non mi meraviglio che sia finito cosí. Ricordo *quanto filo da torcere ha sempre dato* ai suoi genitori. (I'm not surprised he ended up this way. I remember what a hard time he used to give his parents.)

Raccontare per filo e per segno: To give a blow-by-blow account.
LIT. To tell by thread and sign.

FINESTRA (LA) Window

Far la finestra sul tetto a qualcuno: To make love to someone's wife.
LIT. To make a window on someone's roof.

Poveraccio, dicono che quel mascalzone di X *gli faccia perfino la finestra sul tetto.* (Poor guy, I've heard that on top of everything else X is even playing around with his wife.)

O mangiar questa minestra o saltar questa finestra: It's either or!
LIT. (It's) either eating this soup or jumping from this window.

Uscire dalla porta e rientrare dalla finestra: To sneak back in through the back door.
LIT. To leave by the door and come back by the window.

Se vuoi veramente liberartene, bisogna che tu agisca con molta energia, perché quello è un tipo che *esce dalla porta e rientra dalla finestra.* (If you really want to get rid of him, you'll have to do it in no uncertain terms, because he's the kind that can always find some way to sneak back in.)

FIOCCO (IL) Ribbon, bow

Coi fiocchi: Extraordinary, first-rate.
LIT. With bows.

Mi ha dato una ramanzina *coi fiocchi!* (He gave me one hell of a talking-to!) Ho un raffreddore *coi fiocchi!* (I have a first-class cold!)

FIORE (IL) Flower

A fior di labbra (See also **a mezza Bocca**): Unwillingly, half-heartedly, perfunctorily.
LIT. At lips' surface.

Fior di mascalzone: A first-class rat.
LIT. Flower of a rascal.

Fior di quattrini: A lot of money, a pretty penny.
LIT. Flower of money.

Hanno *fior di quattrini,* possono permetterselo. (They're loaded, they can afford it.) Tienlo da conto, mi è costato *fior di quattrini.* (Treasure it, it cost me an arm and a leg.)

Il fior fiore di: The cream of the crop; la crème de la crème.
LIT. The flower flower of.

Nervi a fior di pelle: Nerves on edge.
LIT. Nerves at skin's surface.

FLAGRANTE Flagrant, evident

Cogliere in flagrante: To catch someone in the act, red-handed.
LIT. To catch someone in evident (misdeed).

FOGLIA (LA) Leaf

Mangiar la foglia: To see through a situation, or someone's words or actions.
LIT. To eat the leaf.

Finalmente *ho mangiato la foglia!* Non è l'amore per la poesia che ti spinge a queste conferenze, ma la speranza d'incontrare una certa ragazza. (It took me a while, but I finally caught on! It's not love of poetry that brings you to the lectures, it's hope of meeting a certain girl.)

Mangiar la foglia

FORCA (LA) Pitchfork, gallows

Far forca: To play hooky.
LIT. To do pitchfork.

FORCHETTA (LA) Fork

Essere una buona forchetta: To be a hearty eater.
LIT. To be a good fork.

Parlare in punta di forchetta: To speak with affected elegance.
LIT. To speak on the point of a fork.

Non mi sento a mio agio con lui. Quel suo *parlare in punta di forchetta* mi dà ai nervi. (I don't feel comfortable with him. His tea-and-crumpet manner gets on my nerves.)

FORSE Maybe

Essere in forse: To be of two minds.
LIT. To be in maybe.

FORTUNA (LA) Luck

Afferrare la fortuna per i capelli: To anticipate and be prepared for any favorable opportunity.
LIT. To grasp luck by the hair.

FORZA (LA) Force, strength

A forza di: By dint of; by means of.
LIT. By force of.

A forza di preghiere, è riuscito a dissuaderlo. (It took her days of begging to talk him out of it.)

Bella forza: Big deal!
LIT. Beautiful strength.

Ha dato cento dollari? *Bella forza!* È ricco sfondato! (He donated a hundred dollars? How generous! With all his money . . .)

FOSSA (LA) Hole, grave

Scavarsi la fossa con le proprie mani: To dig one's own grave, to be one's own downfall.
LIT. To dig one's own grave with one's own hands.

FOSSO (IL) Ditch

Saltare il fosso: To take a decisive step.
LIT. To jump the ditch.

Ahimé, *ho saltato il fosso!* Le ho chiesto di sposarmi. (There's no way back, alas! I've asked her to marry me.)

FRANCO Frank, free

Farla franca (See also **passarla Liscia**): To get away with something.
LIT. To do it free.

FRANGIA (LA) Fringe

Fare la frangia: To add to a story; to embellish it with little concern for veracity.
LIT. To make the fringe.

FRATE (**IL**) Friar, monk

In compagnia prese moglie un frate: Nothing is impossible in good company.
LIT. In company a friar took a wife.

> Che importa se non sei mai andato a pescare in vita tua? *In compagnia prese moglie un frate!* (What difference does it make if you've never been fishing before? It will be fun just being together!)

Star coi frati e zappar l'orto: To have no preference; to be willing to follow the group's mood and decisions.
LIT. To stay with the friars and work the orchard.

> Decidete voi. Io *sto coi frati e zappo l'orto.* (You decide. I'll go along with any plan you make.)

FRENO (**IL**) Brake

Mordere il freno: To chafe at the bit.
LIT. To bite the brake.

Star coi frati *e* zappar *l'orto*

FRESCO Cool, fresh

Andare al fresco: To go to jail, to the "cooler."
LIT. To go to the cool.

Star fresco: To be in a fine fix.
LIT. To stay cool.

> Se aspetti che sia lui a chiamarti, *stai fresco!* (If you're waiting for him to call you, don't hold your breath!) Se ti vede Papà, *stai fresco!* (If Daddy sees you, you'll get it!)

FRITTATA (**LA**) Omelette

Fare la frittata: To make a mess, to blunder; to let the cat out of the bag.
LIT. To make the omelette.

Ha detto proprio così? *È fatta la frittata!* (Did he really say that? God, how are we ever going to get out of this one?)

Voltare la frittata (See also **cambiar le Carte in tavola**): To change the meaning of something previously stated.
LIT. To turn the omelette.

FUMO (IL) Smoke

Andare in fumo: To come to nothing; to fizzle.
LIT. To go in smoke.

Aver qualcuno come il fumo agli occhi: Not to be able to stand the sight of someone.
LIT. To have someone like smoke to the eyes.

Molto fumo e poco arrosto: All bones and no meat.
LIT. Much smoke and little roast.

A sentir lui, ha fatto e visto un monte di cose, ma stringi stringi, *molto fumo e poco arrosto.* (To hear him talk, he's had all kinds of experiences, but when you come right down to it I think it's mostly talk.)

Vendere fumo, essere un venditore di fumo: To claim non-existent assets; to be a fraud.
LIT. To sell smoke, to be a smoke salesman.

Non gli dare retta, per carità. Quello è *un venditore di fumo.* (Don't listen to him, for God's sake! He'd try to sell you the Brooklyn Bridge.)

FUOCO (IL) Fire

Buttare olio sul fuoco: Add fuel to the flames, fat to the fire.
LIT. To throw oil on the fire.

Cavar le castagne dal fuoco con la zampa del gatto (See **Gatto**)

Essere tra due fuochi: To be between two fires.

Far fuoco e fiamme: To raise hell, the roof.
LIT. To make fire and flames.

Fuoco di fila: Running fire, barrage.
LIT. Fire in line.

> È stato un *fuoco di fila* di domande, che ha messo alla prova la sua presenza di spirito. (The whole thing was one long barrage of questions that really put his poise to the test.)

Fuoco di paglia (See **Paglia**)

Giuocare col fuoco, scherzare col fuoco: To play with fire.

Mettere a ferro e fuoco: To pillage; to devastate.
LIT. To put through iron and fire.

Mettere la mano sul fuoco: To be willing to stake one's life on something.
LIT. To put one's hand on the fire.

> Quella ragazza è incapace di un'azione simile. *Ci metterei la mano sul fuoco.* (That girl is absolutely incapable of doing such a thing. I'd stake my life on it.)

Mettere l'esca accanto al fuoco, mettere la paglia accanto al fuoco: To expose oneself or others to temptation or danger.
LIT. To put the tinder next to the fire, to put the straw next to the fire.

> Gli dispiace che si sposi così giovane! Ma se è stato lui che *ha messo l'esca accanto al fuoco* chiedendogli di darle lezioni di lingua! (He didn't want her to get married so young! Well, he has only himself to blame. Wasn't he the one who wanted her to take language lessons from that young man?)

Mettere troppa carne al fuoco (See **Carne**)

Pigliar fuoco come l'esca: To be quick to anger; to flare up.
LIT. To catch fire like tinder.

Soffiare sul fuoco: To fan the flames.
LIT. To blow on the fire.

Versare acqua sul fuoco: To calm down flaring tempers; to soothe ruffled feathers.
LIT. To throw water on the fire.

Ma tu perché non sei intervenuto *versando un po' d'acqua sul fuoco?* (But why didn't you step in and at least try to talk some sense into them?)

FUORI Out, outside

Esser fuori di sé dalla rabbia, dalla gioia, ecc.: To be beside oneself with anger, joy, etc.
LIT. To be outside oneself with anger, joy, etc.

Far fuori qualcuno: To do someone in; to get him out of the way.
LIT. To do someone out.

Fuori mano, fuori di mano: Remote, out-of-the-way.
LIT. Outside hand.

È una bella casetta, forse un po' *fuori mano.* (It's a nice little house, though perhaps a little hard to get to.)

FURIA (LA) Fury, haste

In fretta e furia: In disorderly haste.
LIT. In hurry and haste.

Scusami se sono in questo stato, ma son dovuto uscire *in fretta e furia* perché X strepitava giù in strada col claxon come un disperato! (Please forgive the way I look, but I had to rush out of the house because X was downstairs blowing the horn like mad!)

Salire su tutte le furie: To hit the ceiling.
LIT. To climb on all furies.

G

GALERA (LA) Jail

Avanzo di galera: Scoundrel; gangster; scum of the earth.
LIT. Leftover from jail.

GALLO (IL) Rooster

Fare il galletto: To be cocky, to strut, especially with the ladies.
LIT. To do (play) the little rooster.

Non è buono ad altro che a *fare il galletto* con le signore. (The only thing he's good for is to play the ladies' man.)

Gallo della Checca: Cock of the walk.
LIT. Checca's rooster.

Tanti galli a cantar non fa mai giorno: Too many cooks

spoil the broth.

LIT. (When there are) so many cocks singing, day never breaks.

GAMBA (LA) Leg

Correre a gambe levate: To run at full speed; as fast as one can.

LIT. To run at raised legs.

È bastato che chiamassi il cane e quelli via, *a gambe levate!* (All I had to do was call the dog, and they took off as fast as their legs could carry them!)

Tanti galli a cantar non fa mai giorno

Darsela a gambe: To take to one's heels.

LIT. To give oneself to legs.

Drizzare le gambe ai cani (see **Cane**)

Essere in gamba: To feel in fine form; to be on the ball.
LIT. To be in leg.

Conosci X? Quello sì che è un ragazzo *in gamba!* (Do you know X? He's really a very sharp guy!)

Fare il passo più lungo della gamba: To bite off more than one can chew (used mainly in connection with finances).
LIT. To make the step longer than the leg.

Dio voglia che con quell'appartamento *non abbiano fatto il passo più lungo della gamba.* (I hope for their sake they knew what they were doing when they took that apartment.)

Prendere qualcosa sotto gamba (See also **buttarsi qualcosa dietro le Spalle**): To let something slide; not to take it seriously.

LIT. To take something under leg.

GAMBERO (IL) Shrimp, crab

Progresso da gambero: No progress at all.
LIT. Crab-like progress.

Rosso come un gambero: Red as a beet (said of someone who is deeply embarrassed and confused).
LIT. Red as a shrimp.

GATTO (IL) Cat

Avere altre gatte da pelare: To have more important things on one's mind; to have other fish to fry.
LIT. To have other cats to skin.

Avere un occhio alla gatta e uno alla padella: To take care of two different and conflicting things at the same time.
LIT. To have one eye to the cat and one to the frying pan.

Cavar le castagne dal fuoco con la zampa del gatto: To let someone else do the dirty work while reaping the benefits; to make a cat's-paw of someone.
LIT. To pull the chestnuts out of the fire with the cat's-paw.

Lui spera che sia io a portare la questione sul tappeto, ma si sbaglia se spera di usare *la mia zampa per cavare dal fuoco le sue castagne.* (He hopes that I'm going to be the one to bring up the matter. He's out of his mind if he thinks I'm going to risk my neck to protect his interests!)

Comprare la gatta nel sacco: To buy a pig in a poke.
LIT. To buy the cat in the bag.

Far la gatta morta: To play possum.
LIT. To do (play) the dead cat.

Gatta ci cova: There's something fishy going on!
LIT. Cat is nesting there.

Se è gentile con te, *gatta ci cova!* (If she's that nice to you, I smell a rat!)

Pigliarsi una gatta a pelare: To take on a difficult and un-rewarding enterprise.
LIT. To take oneself a cat to skin.

Si è preso una bella gatta a pelare! (Lord, what a job he saddled himself with!)

Quando il gatto è fuori i sorci ballano: When the cat's away the mice will play.
LIT. When the cat is out the mice dance.

Quattro gatti: Scanty attendance.
LIT. Four cats.

Serata moscissima! Eravamo quattro gatti. (A deadly evening! Hardly a soul there.)

GAVETTA (LA) Mess tin

Venire dalla gavetta: To be a self-made man, to rise from the ranks.
LIT. To come from the mess tin.

GHIACCIO (IL) Ice

Rompere il ghiaccio: To break the ice.

GIACOMO James

Fare Giacomo Giacomo: To have one's knees knock, turn to water.
LIT. To do James James (said of legs).

Mentre aspettavo, le gambe mi facevano Giacomo Giacomo. (While I was standing there waiting, my knees were shaking like mad.)

GIOIA (LA) Joy

Darsi alla pazza gioia: To go on a spree; to have a fling.
LIT. To give oneself to crazy joy.

Non stare in sé dalla gioia: To be beside oneself with joy.
LIT. Not to stay within oneself from joy.

Hai visto X? *Non sta in sé dalla gioia*—ha vinto alle corse. (Have you seen X? He's bursting with joy—he won at the races.)

GIORNO (IL) Day

Avere i giorni contati: To be doomed.
LIT. To have the days counted.

> *Ha i giorni contati.* (His days are numbered.)

Essere all'ordine del giorno: To happen constantly, said especially of unpleasant things.
LIT. To be at the order of the day (on the agenda).

> Se vedessi il bambino! I capricci in casa loro *sono all'ordine del giorno.* (You should see their kid! In their house tantrums are the rule.)

Oggigiorno: Nowadays; in this day and age.

Vivere alla giornata: To live from day to day.
LIT. To live at the day.

GIRARE To turn

Girare a: To feel a sudden whim to do or say something.
LIT. To turn to.

> Che *ti gira?* (What's come over you?)

Gli è girato così: He must have felt like doing it; he took it into his head to do it.
LIT. It turned to him this way.

GIRO (IL) Turn

Prendere in giro: To tease; to make fun of; to pull someone's leg.
LIT. To take around.

GIUDIZIO (IL) Wisdom

Mettere giudizio: To wise up; to sober down.
LIT. To put on wisdom.

Ti puoi fidare di me. *Ho messo giudizio!* (You can trust me. I've learned my lesson by now.)

Mettere giudizio a qualcuno: To teach someone a lesson.
LIT. To put wisdom to someone.

GIUOCO or GIOCO (IL) Game, play

A che giuoco si giuoca: What's going on here?
LIT. What game are we playing?

Aver buon giuoco: To hold all the cards.
LIT. To have good play.

Capirai, i furbi di quel tipo *hanno buon giuoco* con donne ingenue come lei. (A sweet, naive woman like her can't help being easy prey for schemers of his kind.)

Chi sa il giuoco non lo insegni: Don't let anyone in on your secret methods, or you will be unable to use them any longer.
LIT. He who knows the game shouldn't teach it.

Far buon viso a cattivo giuoco: To grin and bear it; to make the best of a bad bargain.
LIT. To show good face to bad game.

Far giuoco: To come in handy.
LIT. To make game.

Sperava d'imbarazzarmi, ma invece quel che ha detto *mi fa giuoco.* (He wanted to embarrass me, but the things he said were all to my advantage.)

Farsi giuoco di qualcuno: To pull the wool over someone's eyes.
LIT. To make game of someone.

Fare il doppio giuoco: To play a double game.

Fare il giuoco di qualcuno: To play into someone's hands.
LIT. To make the game of someone.

Non capisci che ad arrabbiarti in questo modo, *fai esattamente il suo giuoco?* (Don't you see that if you get mad you're falling right into his trap?)

Giuoco di società: Parlor game.
LIT. Society's game.

Il giuoco non vale la candela: The game isn't worth the candle.

In giuoco: At stake.
LIT. In game.

Stare al giuoco: To be game.
LIT. To stay at the game.

GOCCIA (LA) Drop

La goccia che fa traboccare il vaso: The straw that broke the camel's back.
LIT. The drop that makes the vase overflow.

Somigliarsi come due gocce d'acqua: To be like two peas in a pod.
LIT. To resemble each other like two drops of water.

GOLA (LA) Throat

A gola spiegata: At the top of one's lungs.
LIT. At unfolded throat.

A squarciagola: At the top of one's voice.
LIT. At splitting throat.

Mentire per la gola: To lie in one's teeth.
LIT. To lie in one's throat.

Prendere qualcuno per la gola: To get to someone through his love for food.
LIT. To take someone by the throat.

> Non voleva venire, ma *l'ho preso per la gola* e non ha saputo resistere all'idea delle tue scaloppine. (He didn't want to come, but I knew he wouldn't be able to resist the idea of your veal cutlets.)

GOMITO (IL) Elbow

Alzare il gomito: To get high; to bend the elbow.
LIT. To lift the elbow.

Alzare il gomito

Olio di gomito: Elbow grease.
LIT. Elbow's oil.

GRANA (LA) Nuisance

Piantar grane, piantare una grana: To stir up trouble.
LIT. To plant nuisances; to plant a nuisance.

Grazie per avermi presentato quel tuo amico! *Mi ha piantato una di quelle grane . . .* (Thanks a lot for sending that friend of yours over. He stirred up a hornet's nest none of us is likely to forget!)

GRAZIA (LA) Grace

Essere fuori dalla grazia di Dio (See **Dio**)

Essere nelle buone grazie di qualcuno: To be in someone's good graces.

GRILLO (IL) Cricket

Aver grilli per il capo: To be a flighty, unreliable person.
LIT. To have crickets in one's head.

Sarà simpaticissima, ma per quel posto non va bene. *Ha troppi grilli per il capo.* (I'm sure she's a lovely girl, but she's not right for the job. Too many bees in her bonnet.)

Indovinala grillo! (See also **vattela Pesca**): Your guess is as good as mine!
LIT. Guess it cricket!

Chi poi sia stato a mettergli quell'idea in testa, *indovinala grillo!* (God only knows who put that idea in his head!)

GRINZA (LA) Wrinkle

Non fare una grinza: To be flawless.
LIT. Not to make a wrinkle.

Devo ammettere che il suo ragionamento *non faceva una grinza.* (I have to admit that his argument was irrefutable.)

GROSSO Big

Dirne delle grosse, spararle grosse: To talk big; to make grossly inaccurate statements; to tell tall tales.
LIT. To say them big; to shoot them big.

Ma lo sai che certe volte *ne dici delle grosse?* (Sometimes you really say the most incredible things!)

Farla grossa: To put one's big foot in it.
LIT. To make it big.

Questa volta *l'ha fatta grossa!* (He really did it this time!)

GUANTO (IL) Glove

Gettare il guanto, raccogliere il guanto: To throw down the gauntlet; to take up the gauntlet.

Ladro in guanti gialli: Gentleman thief.
LIT. Thief in yellow gloves.

Mano di ferro in guanto di velluto: To tread softly and carry a big stick.
LIT. Iron hand in velvet glove.

Ti sta come un guanto novo: It serves you right!
LIT. It fits you like a new glove.

Trattare qualcuno coi guanti: To handle someone with (kid) gloves.

GUSTO (IL) Taste

De gustibus non est disputandum: (Latin for) There's no arguing with taste.

Non capisco perché ti ci arrabbi. *De gustibus . . .* (I don't know why you get so mad at him. To each his own . . .)

Tutti i gusti son gusti: Everyone is entitled to his own taste.
LIT. All tastes are tastes.

I

IMBECCATA (L') Feeding (said of birds, chickens, etc.)

Dare l'imbeccata: To suggest answers; to prompt.
LIT. To give the feeding.

Ti assicuro che è capacissimo di cavarsela da solo, senza che tu *gli dia l'imbeccata*. (He's quite capable of taking care of himself, I assure you. There's no need for you to spoon-feed him the answers.)

INCUDINE (L') Anvil

Essere tra l'incudine e il martello: To be between the devil and the deep blue sea.
LIT. To be between the anvil and the hammer.

INDIANO (L') Indian

Fare l'indiano (See also fare **Orecchi da mercante**): To turn a deaf ear. LIT. To do the Indian.

Fila indiana: Indian file, single file.

INVENTARIO (L') Inventory

Con beneficio d'inventario: Originally a purely legal term—the right to have an inventory of the estate's assets when accepting a legacy; now with reservations, with a grain of salt.

Fare l'indiano

Non te la prendere! Sai bene che le dichiarazioni di X vanno sempre prese *con beneficio d'inventario*. (Don't get yourself all worked up! You know that X's statements must always be taken with a grain of salt.)

L

LA (**IL**) A (musical pitch)

Dare il la: To set the tone.
LIT. To give the A.

Per fortuna ci sarà X a *dare il la* alla conversazione. (Fortunately X will be there to bring up an interesting subject.)

Prendere il la: To take the lead from someone.
LIT. To take the A.

LABBRO (**IL**) Lip

A fior di labbra (See **Fiore**)

Leccarsi le labbra (See also **leccarsi le Dita, i Baffi**): To lick one's chops.

LIT. To lick one's lips.

Mordersi le labbra: To bite back one's anger or annoyance.
LIT. To bite one's lips.

> *Mi son morso le labbra,* perché, t'assicuro, si sarebbe meritato una risposta di quelle pepate! (I really had to bite my lips to keep from telling him off as he deserved!)

Pendere dalle labbra di: To hang on the lips of.

LACRIMA (LA) Tear

Aver le lacrime in pelle in pelle: To be very close to tears.
LIT. To have tears in skin in skin.

> Mi ha detto che non ti ha ringraziato perché *aveva le lacrime in pelle in pelle* e temeva di scoppiare in sighiozzi. (She told me she couldn't thank you because she was on the verge of tears and was terribly afraid she'd burst out crying.)

Aver le lacrime in tasca: To cry easily.
LIT. To have tears in one's pocket.

Lacrime di cocodrillo: Crocodile tears.

LADRO (IL) Thief

Buio da ladri: Pitch dark.
LIT. Dark for thieves.

Essere come i ladri di Pisa (che di giorno litigano e la notte rubano insieme): To be partners in crime, mischief.
LIT. To be like the thieves of Pisa (who quarrel by day and at night get together to steal).

> Che ragazzacci! Mi fanno disperare coi loro eterni litigi, ma quando si tratta di marachelle . . . *veri ladri di Pisa!* (Those boys drive me crazy! They fight all day long but when there's mischief in the air, they're thick as thieves!)

Ladro in guanti gialli (See **Guanto**)

L'occasione fa l'uomo ladro: Opportunity makes the thief.

LAMPO (IL) Lightning

Lampo di genio: Stroke of genius; brainstorm.
LIT. Lightning of genius.

LANA (LA) Wool

Andar per lana e tornarsene tosi (See also **Pifferi di montagna**): To go for wool and come home shorn.

Buona lana: He's a fine one! (sarcastic)
LIT. Good wool.

Questioni di lana caprina: Pointless, futile arguments.
LIT. Arguments (made) of goat's wool.

LANCIA (LA) Lance, spear

Spezzare una lancia in favore di qualcuno: To rise in defense of someone; to make a statement in support of something or someone.
LIT. To break a lance on behalf of someone.

C'è nessuno che voglia *spezzare una lancia* in favore di questa proposta? (Does anyone want to go to bat for this proposal?)

LARGO (IL) Open

Prendere il largo: To escape from justice, or, at least, from trouble.
LIT. To take to the open (sea).

Ho paura che i tuoi soldi non li rivedrai per un pezzo. Quello *ha preso il largo* e chi lo trova è bravo. (I'm afraid you won't see your money again for quite a while. Your man has taken off and God only knows where he is by now.)

LEGGE (LA) Law

Fatta la legge trovato l'inganno: As soon as the law is made, loopholes are found.
LIT. Made the law found the deception.

LEPRE (LA) Hare

Invitare la lepre a correre (See also **invitare qualcuno a Nozze**): To ask someone to do something he is especially eager or well-equipped to do.
LIT. To invite the hare to run.

LETTO (IL) Bed

Cascare dal letto: Said of a lazy person when he gets up unusually early.
LIT. To fall from the bed.

Guarda chi si vede! *Sei cascato dal letto?* (Look who's here! What on earth got you up at this hour?)

Essere fra letto e lettuccio: To be in poor health.
LIT. To be between bed and cot.

Mia madre? Purtroppo sempre *tra letto e lettuccio.* (My mother? Unfortunately, she hardly ever gets out of bed these days.)

LEVARE To remove, to raise

Fare una levataccia (See also **fare un'Alzataccia**): To get up at an ungodly hour.
LIT. To make an awful rising.

Fare una levataccia a qualcuno (See also **fare un'Alzataccia a qualcuno**): To jump down someone's throat; to give him a sharp reply.
LIT. To make an awful rising at someone.

M'ha fatto una levataccia, come se—invece di una domanda innocente—avessi commesso chissà che indiscrezione. (He jumped at me as if I had been guilty of God knows what crime, instead of a harmless question.)

Levarsi il pensiero: To get something over with.
LIT. To take away the thought.

Levarsi qualcosa dalla testa: To put something out of one's mind.

LIT. To remove something from one's head.

Levatelo dalla testa! (Not a chance!)

Levata di scudi (See also **Alzata di scudi**): Sudden protest or act of rebellion.
LIT. Raising of shields.

Non vedo la ragione di questa *levata di scudi.* (I don't see any reason for this sudden show of righteous indignation.)

LÌ, LÀ There

Essere lì lì per: To be just about to, to be on the verge of.
LIT. To be there there to.

Son stato lì lì per dirgli quel che pensavo di lui. (I was on the verge of giving him a piece of my mind.)

Giù di lì: About that time; thereabouts; circa.
LIT. Down of there.

Saranno state le otto o *giù di lì.* (It must have been eight o'clock or thereabouts.)

Lì per lì: Then and there; at the time.
LIT. There for there.

Lì per lì non ho saputo che cosa rispondere. (At the time I was left speechless.) Ho deciso di partire *lì per lì.* (Then and there, I decided to go.)

Essere più di là che di qua: To be close to death.
LIT. To be more on the other than on this side.

LIBRO (IL) Book

Essere nel libro di qualcuno, non essere nel libro di qualcuno: To be in good with someone, to be in bad with someone.
LIT. To be in someone's book, not to be in someone's book.

Essere un libro chiuso: Said of a person whose behavior is a puzzle, who is unpredictable.
LIT. To be a closed book.

Per me, quella ragazza *è sempre stata un libro chiuso.* (As far as I'm concerned, I've never been able to figure her out.)

Libro giallo, romanzo giallo: Mystery, thriller.
LIT. Yellow book, yellow novel.

Parlare come un libro stampato: To make a great deal of sense (said teasingly of someone whose words are a bit pompous).
LIT. To talk like a printed book.

Bravissimo! *Parli come un libro stampato!* (Good for you! You know, you make a lot of sense today.)

LINGUA (LA) Tongue

Aver la lingua lunga: To be prone to gossip.
LIT. To have a long tongue.

Avere la lingua sciolta: To be articulate, glib.
LIT. To have a loose tongue.

Avere qualcosa sulla punta della lingua: To have something on the tip of one's tongue.

Avere una lingua che taglia e cuce: To have a very sharp tongue.
LIT. To have a tongue that cuts and sews.

Essere una cattiva lingua, essere una linguaccia: To be a scandal-monger, an ugly gossip.
LIT. To be a bad tongue.

Essere una lingua sacrilega: To have a blasphemous tongue; to be a scandal-monger.
LIT. To be a sacrilegious tongue.

Lapsus linguae: Slip of the tongue.
LIT. (Latin for) Error of the tongue.

Scusami tanto, sapevo benissimo che era medico. È stato *un lapsus.* (I'm so sorry. Of course I knew he was a doctor —it was just a slip of the tongue.)

Mordersi la lingua: To feel like kicking oneself for something said.
LIT. To bite one's tongue.

Mi son morso la lingua, ma ahimé troppo tardi! (I could have bitten off my tongue, but it was too late, the words were out!)

Ne ferisce più la lingua che la spada: Slander is deadlier than the sword.
LIT. The tongue wounds more of them than the sword.

Non aver peli sulla lingua (See **Pelo**)

Sentirsi prudere la lingua: To have a strong urge to talk; to itch to say something.
LIT. To feel one's tongue itch.

Mi sentivo prudere la lingua, sai, ma ho pensato a te e preferito esser prudente. (I really was dying to say something, you know, but I thought of you and decided it was best to be careful.)

LISCIO Smooth

Andare per le lisce: To go smoothly, like clockwork.
LIT. To go for the smooth ones.

Andar liscio come l'olio (See **Olio**)

Passarla liscia (See also **farla Franca**): To get away with something.
LIT. To pass it smooth.

Passarla liscia a qualcuno: To let someone off the hook.
LIT. To pass it smooth to someone.

Tu, però, sei esagerato. *Non gliene passi una liscia!* (You really go overboard, you never let him get away with a thing!)

LODE (LA) Praise

Cantar le lodi di qualcuno, tessere le lodi di qualcuno: To sing someone's praises.

Cantar le proprie lodi: To blow one's own horn.
LIT. To sing one's own praises

LUCCIOLA (LA) Firefly

Prendere lucciole per lanterne (See also **prender fischi per Fiaschi**): To be grossly deceived by appearances.

LIT. To mistake fireflies for lanterns.

LUME (IL) Lamp, light

A lume di naso (See **Naso**)

Prendere lucciole *per lanterne*

A questi lumi di luna: At this critical time.
LIT. At these lights of the moon.

Chiedere denari a mio padre, *a questi lumi di luna?* Fossi matto! (Ask my father for money with business the way it is these days? I'd have to be crazy!)

Essere al lumicino: To be breathing one's last.
LIT. To be at the little lamp.

Perdere il lume degli occhi: To lose one's temper; to hit the ceiling.
LIT. To lose the light of one's eyes.

Reggere il lume: To play a reluctant chaperone.
LIT. To hold the lamp.

È stata una serata noiosissima. Era chiaro che quei due se l'intendevano, e a me è toccato *reggere il lume.* (It was a deadly evening. There was obviously something going on between them, and I felt like a fifth wheel.)

Reggere il lume

LUNA (LA) Moon

Abbaiare alla luna: To engage in futile protests.
LIT. To bark at the moon.

Alzarsi con la luna di traverso: To get up on the wrong side of bed.
LIT. To get up with the moon upside down.

Avere le lune: To be moody, irritable.
LIT. To have the moons.

Essere nel mondo della luna: To be lost in reverie; a million miles away.
LIT. To be in the world of the moon.

Far veder la luna nel pozzo: To deceive someone with illusory assurances.
LIT. To show someone the moon in the well.

No, mio caro. A me *non fai vedere la luna nel pozzo!* (No, sir. You're not going to sell me a bill of goods!)

Venire dal mondo della luna: To be astonishingly uninformed about a given subject; to be out of it.
LIT. To come from the world of the moon.

LUNARIO (IL) Almanac

Sbarcare il lunario: To barely make ends meet.
LIT. To land the almanac.

LUNGO Long

Andare per le lunghe: To take more time than expected.
LIT. To go for the long ones.

Farla lunga: To make a production out of something.
LIT. To make it long.

Non farla tanto lunga! Dopo tutto, non si tratta che di un raffreddore. (Don't make such a big deal out of it! So you have a cold!)

Saperla lunga: To be a smart cookie, to be an old hand at something.
LIT. To know it long.

LUPO (IL) Wolf

Chi pecora si fa lupo la mangia: He who behaves like a sheep gets eaten by the wolf.

In bocca al lupo: A way of wishing good luck, originally said only in connection with hunting; now used on a variety of occasions.
LIT. In the wolf's mouth.

Il tuo esame è domani, vero? *In bocca al lupo!* (Your exam is tomorrow, isn't it? Good luck, then!)

In bocca al lupo

Lupus in fabula: The very person; speak of the devil.
LIT. (Latin for) Wolf in the story.

O guarda, *lupus in fabula!* Si parlava del tuo incidente automobilistico. (Look who just came in! We were talking about your car accident.)

M

MA But

Macché: Strong negative expression, such as: not in the least; far from it; I should say not.
LIT. But what.

"Ti ha poi telefonato quel tale?" "*Macché,* non si è più fatto vivo!" ("Did that fellow ever call you?" "Not a chance, I never heard from him again.") *Macché investimento!* Son denari buttati via, te lo dico io. (Investment, my eye! It's all money down the drain, that's what it is!)

Non c'è ma che tenga: I won't take no for an answer.
LIT. There is no but that holds.

MACCHIA (LA) Thicket, stain

Alla macchia: Clandestinely.

LIT. At the thicket.

Era un giornale stampato *alla macchia* da un gruppo di intellettuali antifascisti. (It was an undercover paper printed by a group of anti-fascist intellectuals.)

Darsi alla macchia: To go into hiding; to take to the woods.
LIT. To give oneself to the thicket.

MAGGIORE Greater, greatest

Andare per la maggiore: To be the most prominent in one's field.
LIT. To go for the greatest.

E un attore che a me piace fino a un certo punto, ma *va per la maggiore.* (I'm not too enthusiastic about him as an actor, but he's certainly one of the most popular today.)

MALATTIA (LA) Illness, disease

Farne una malattia: To take something very much to heart; to get sick over it.
LIT. To make an illness of it.

MALE (IL) Evil, harm

MALE Badly

Mal comune mezzo gaudio: Company in distress makes sorrow less; or, misery loves company.
LIT. Common evil half joy.

Male in arnese: Shabbily dressed; down at the heels.
LIT. Badly in tool.

Quel tuo amico mi sembra un po' *male in arnese.* (That friend of yours looks a little seedy to me.)

Male malanno e uscio addosso: All possible misfortunes.
LIT. Pain, sorrow, and the door on top.

Poveraccio! Ha proprio *male malanno e uscio addosso!* (Poor guy, everything seems to happen to him!)

Male non fare paura non avere: Do no harm, have no fear.

Meno male: Thank goodness.
LIT. Less bad.

Una borsa di studio? *Meno male!* Almeno potrà risolvere i problemi più urgenti. (A fellowship? Thank goodness for that! At least he'll be able to take care of his most pressing needs.)

Metter male: To introduce discord; to make trouble.
LIT. To put evil.

Non credo ci sia un briciolo di verità in quel che dice. Lo sai che gli piace di *metter male.* (I don't think there's an ounce of truth in what he says. You know he enjoys nothing more than getting people mad at each other!)

Mettersi male: To take a turn for the worse.
LIT. To put itself bad.

Mi pare che le cose *si mettano male.* (Things look pretty bad to me.)

Non c'è male: Not bad.
LIT. There is no evil.

"Com'è andata la serata?" "*Non c'è male.*" ("How did the evening go?" "It could have been worse.")

Non tutto il male viene per nuocere: Some clouds have a silver lining.
LIT. Not all sorrow comes to bring damage.

Non tutto il male viene per nuocere: questa malattia m'ha dato la possibilità di mettermi a giorno degli ultimi periodici legali. (This illness has really been a blessing in disguise, because I've had a chance to catch up on all the legal journals.)

Prendersela a male: To take something amiss; to take offense at it.
LIT. To take something to the bad.

Rimaner male: To feel bad; to be embarrassed, disappointed.
LIT. To remain badly.

Dì la verità che *ci sei rimasto male.* (Come on, admit you were disappointed.)

MANCARE To lack, to miss

Ci mancava anche questa: We needed this like a hole in the head!
LIT. This too was missing.

Ci mancherebbe altro: Perish the thought! That's all we need!
LIT. That would be missing from it.

Mancare un venerdì: To be touched in the head; to have a screw loose.
LIT. To lack a Friday.

È simpatico, ma non si può mai sapere quel che farà. Ho l'impressione che *gli manchi un venerdì!* (He's nice, but you never know what he'll do next. I have the feeling he's a little on the nutty side.)

MANDARE To send

Mandare a quel paese, mandare al diavolo, mandare a farsi benedire, mandare a farsi friggere: To tell someone off; to send him packing; to tell him to go to the devil.
LIT. To send to that country, to the devil; to get blessed; to get fried.

Mandare qualcuno da Erode a Pilato: To send someone from pillar to post.
LIT. To send someone from Herod to Pilate.

Non mandarle a dire: Not to mince words.
LIT. Not to send them to say.

Quello è un tipo che *non le manda a dire.* (He doesn't pull any punches.)

MANICA (LA) Sleeve

Avere un asso nella manica (See **Asso**)

Essere di manica *larga*

Essere di manica larga: To be lenient, broad-minded, generous.
LIT. To be of large sleeve.

Posso rientrare all'ora che mi pare. In queste cose i miei genitori *sono molto di manica larga.* (I can come in whenever I feel like it. My parents are very lenient about things like that.)

Essere di manica stretta: To be stingy, narrow-minded.
LIT. To be of narrow sleeve.

Un altro paio di maniche: A horse of another color.
LIT. Another pair of sleeves.

MANICO (IL) Handle

Avere il coltello dalla parte del manico: To have the upper hand.
LIT. To have the knife by the handle end.

Allo stato attuale delle cose, posso fare ben poco. Che vuoi, *ha il coltello dalla parte del manico.* (As things stand now, there's very little I can do. He's got me over a barrel.)

Ciurlare nel manico: To waver in carrying out a promise, an agreement.
LIT. To shift in the handle.

Gettare il manico dietro la scure: To cause small things to deteriorate out of desperation at the loss of more important ones.
LIT. To throw the handle after the axe.

Tu vorresti *gettare il manico dietro la scure,* ma devi invece cercare di salvare tutto il possibile. (You feel like letting everything go down the drain, but you have to try to salvage what you can.)

Il difetto è nel manico: It's wrong from the word go.
LIT. The fault is in the handle.

MANO (LA) Hand, coat of paint

Alla mano: Cordial, affable, informal.
LIT. At the hand.

Non aver soggezione di lui. È la persona più *alla mano* di questo mondo. (Don't be awed by him. He's the most easygoing guy in the world.)

Avere la mano felice: To be felicitous in one's choices.
LIT. To have the happy hand.

Hai avuto la mano felice! La segretaria che mi hai trovato è un vero gioiello. (You sure knew what you were doing when you picked that secretary for me! She's a gem.)

Avere le mani bucate: To be a spendthrift.
LIT. To have holes in one's hands.

Purtroppo *ha le mani bucate.* (Unfortunately, money burns a hole in his pocket.)

Avere le mani d'oro: To be a talented, versatile housewife.
LIT. To have hands of gold.

Aver le mani in pasta (See **Pasta**)

Aver le mani in molte paste (See **Pasta**)

Aver le mani legate, essere legato mani e piedi: To have one's hands tied, to be tied hand and foot.

Aver le mani lunghe: To be powerful; occasionally, to be light-fingered.
LIT. To have long hands.

Cogliere qualcuno con le mani nel sacco: To catch someone red-handed.
LIT. To catch someone with his hands in the bag.

Dar l'ultima mano a qualcosa: To put the finishing touches on something.
LIT. To give the last coat to something.

Dar man forte: To come to the rescue.
LIT. To give strong hand.

Dare una mano a qualcuno: To give someone a hand.

Di seconda mano: Second hand.

Fare man bassa: To ransack, rifle.
LIT. To make low hand.

Ho visto che hai *fatto man bassa dei cioccolatini.* (I see you finished off all the candy.)

Forzar la mano a qualcuno: To force someone's hand.

Fuori mano, fuori di mano (See **Fuori**)

Lavarsi le mani di qualcuno o qualcosa: To wash one's hands of someone or something.

Mani di ricotta: Butter-fingers.
LIT. Hands of cottage cheese.

Mano a mano che (See also **Via via che**): As; while; in the process.

Mano a mano che gli parlavo, capivo che non mi avrebbe mai dato retta. (As I was talking to him, I began to realize that he would never take my advice.)

Mano di ferro in guanto di velluto (See **Guanto**)

Mettere le mani avanti: To take steps (especially in the way of statements) to prevent later misunderstandings.

LIT. To put one's hands forward.

> Cos'è? *Metti le mani avanti* in modo che capisca di non poter contar su te? (Are you trying to let me know that I shouldn't count on your help?)

Mettersi le mani nei capelli: To throw up one's hands. LIT. To put one's hands in one's hair.

Mettere le mani *avanti*

Mordersi le mani (See also **mordersi le Dita**): To feel like kicking oneself for something done. LIT. To bite one's hands.

> *Mi mordo le mani* per non aver comprato quella casa quattro anni fa. (I could kick myself for not having bought that house four years ago.)

Non saper dove mettere le mani: To be at a loss in the face of disorder; not to know where to begin. LIT. Not to know where to put one's hands.

Portare qualcuno in palma di mano: To think the world of someone. LIT. To carry someone in the palm of one's hand.

Prendere il coraggio a due mani (See **Coraggio**)

Prender la mano: To take the bit in one's teeth; to get out of hand. LIT. To take the hand.

> Con un gruppo così numeroso ci vuole un insegnante che sappia il fatto suo. Altrimenti *prendono la mano* subito. (With a class that large, you need an experienced teacher or the group gets out of hand immediately.)

Rubare a man salva: To steal without shame or reserve.
LIT. To steal with safe hand.

Sentirsi prudere le mani: To feel like hitting someone; to itch to hit him.
LIT. To feel one's hands itch.

Star con le mani in mano (See also **star con le mani alla Cintola, in Tasca**): To be idle, passive, to stand by with folded hands.
LIT. To stay with one's hands in hand.

> Via, aiutami! Non *startene lì con le mani in mano!* (Come on, give me a hand! Don't just sit there!)

Tener mano a qualcuno: To aid and abet someone's bad deeds.
LIT. To keep hand to someone.

> Non è che io *gli tenga mano,* solo mi rendo conto delle sue condizioni. (Not that I'm giving him any encouragement, it's just that I do understand his position.)

Portare qualcuno in palma di mano

Toccar con mano: To see for oneself.

LIT. To touch with one's hand.

Venire alle mani: To come to blows.
LIT. To come to the hands.

MARCIAPIEDE (IL) Sidewalk

Battere il marciapiede: To be a streetwalker.
LIT. To beat the sidewalk.

MARE (IL) Sea

Essere in alto mare: To be up in the air.
LIT. To be in high sea.

Promettere mari e monti: To promise the moon.
LIT. To promise seas and mountains.

Smuovere mare e monti: To move heaven and earth.
LIT. To move sea and mountains.

Un mare di: A lot of.
LIT. A sea of.

Sono in *un mare di* guai. (I'm up to my ears in trouble.)

MARINAIO (IL) Sailor

Marinaio d'acqua dolce: Person having little aptitude for a given job.
LIT. Sailor fit for sweet (fresh) water.

Promesse da marinaio: Promises made without intending to keep them.
LIT. Sailor's promises.

Ha detto che sarebbe venuto? *Promesse da marinaio!* (What if he *did* promise to come? I wouldn't count on it, if I were you.)

MASTICARE To chew

Masticare amaro: To accept something very reluctantly and resentfully.
LIT. To chew bitter.

Ha finalmente acconsentito a dare le dimissioni, ma *mastica amaro*. (He finally agreed to resign, but he's very bitter about the whole thing.)

MATTINO (IL) Morning

Dal mattino si conosce il buon giorno: You can detect a good day from the morning.

A sei anni, comportarsi a quel modo? Stiamo freschi!

Dal mattino si conosce il buon giorno! (He's only six, and already so demanding? God help us, if this is only the beginning!)

Di buon mattino: Bright and early.
LIT. Of good morning.

Il mattino ha l'oro in bocca: Any job is done better and more easily in the morning.
LIT. The morning has gold in its mouth.

MATTO Crazy

Andar matto per: To go crazy for.

Matto da legare: Mad, utterly irresponsible.
LIT. Crazy to be tied.

Sposarsi, alla sua età? *È matto da legare!* (He's going to get married, at his age? He ought to be in a strait jacket!)

Ne sa più il matto a casa sua che il savio in casa altrui: Regarding the difficulty of preaching, or giving advice, when not personally acquainted with a situation.
LIT. A crazy man knows more in his own house than a wise man in someone else's house.

MAZZO (IL) Bunch

Metter tutti in un mazzo: To make no distinction; to lump together.
LIT. To put everyone in one bunch.

A dir la verità, io *li metto tutti in un mazzo.* (To tell the truth, they're all alike to me.)

MENO Less

In men che non si dica: Quicker than you can say Jack Robinson.
LIT. In less than one can say.

È andato e tornato *in men che non si dica.* (He came and went in no time.)

Parlare del più e del meno (See **Parlare**)

MENTE (LA) Mind

Farci mente locale: To concentrate; to stop and think about something.
LIT. To make local mind on something.

Se *ci fai mente locale,* converrai che tutto faceva prevedere gli avvenimenti di oggi. (If you stop and think about it, you'll agree that everything pointed to what happened today.)

Uscir di mente (See **Uscire**)

MERCATO (IL) Market

A buon mercato: Cheap, inexpensive.
LIT. At good market.

Se l'è cavata *a buon mercato.* (He got off easy.)

Mercato delle vacche: Trading of positions in politics, horse trading.
LIT. Cow market.

Mercato nero: Black market.

Per soprammercato: On top of everything else.
LIT. For over market.

MESTIERE (IL) Trade, job

Chi vuol far l'altrui mestiere rompe l'uova nel paniere: He who wants to do someone else's job, breaks the eggs in the basket (makes a mess of it).

Essere del mestiere: To be well-versed in a given field.
LIT. To be of the trade.

Mi dispiace di non poterti aiutare, ma qui ci vuole uno *del mestiere.* (I'm sorry I can't help you, but this takes a professional.)

Ferri del mestiere: Tools of the trade.

Incerti del mestiere: Occupational hazards; risks of the game.
LIT. Uncertainties of the trade.

MESTOLO (IL) Ladle

Reggere il mestolo: To be in charge; to rule the roost.
LIT. To hold the ladle.

METÀ (LA) Half

La mia metà: My better half.

METTERE To put

Mettere su qualcuno: To get someone worked up about something.
LIT. To put someone up.

> Son sicuro che qualcuno *l'ha messo su,* perché di natura è una persona gentilissima. (I'm sure someone got him all worked up, because otherwise he's the kindest soul on earth.)

Mettersi a tu per tu con qualcuno: To put oneself on the same footing with someone.
LIT. To put oneself at you for you with someone.

> Non puoi *metterti a tu per tu* col tuo principale. (You can't talk to your boss in that tone of voice. He's not your brother, you know!)

Mettersi in ghingheri: To dress up to kill.
LIT. To put oneself in "ghingheri" (used only in this expression).

MEZZO Half, middle

A mezza giornata: Part time.
LIT. At half day.

> Una donna *a mezza giornata.* (A part-time maid.)

Andar di mezzo: To be the fall guy; to bear the brunt.
LIT. To go in the middle.

> Non dirgli che te ne ho parlato io. Non vorrei *ci andasse di mezzo l'amicizia.* (Don't tell him I was the one to mention it. I wouldn't want to jeopardize our friendship.)

Avere una mezza idea di: To have half a mind to.
LIT. To have half an idea to.

Essere mezzo mezzo (See also **essere giù di Corda**): To be under the weather.
LIT. To be half half.

Ma, così, *mezzo mezzo!* (Not so hot!)

Metter in mezzo qualcuno: To take someone in; to deceive him.
LIT. To put someone in middle.

Mettersi di mezzo: To intervene; to act as intermediary.
LIT. To put oneself in middle.

Ti farebbe piacere che *mi ci mettessi di mezzo* io? (Would you like me to try and act as an intermediary?)

Mezzo mondo (See **Mondo**)

Via di mezzo: Happy medium.
LIT. Middle road.

MILLE Thousand

Darla in mille: To challenge someone to guess.
LIT. To give it in thousand.

Sai con chi era X ieri sera a teatro? *Te la dò in mille.* (You know who X was out with last night? You won't guess in a million years!)

MINUTO (IL) Minute

Spaccare il minuto: To keep perfect time; to be absolutely on time.
LIT. To split the minute.

Magnifico, *spacchi il minuto!* (Good for you, you're right on the dot!)

MIRA (LA) Aim

Prendere di mira qualcosa: To make someone the target for one's attacks.
LIT. To aim at someone.

MIRABILIA (Latin for) Wonders

Dire mirabilia di qualcuno o qualcosa: To have the most wonderful things to say about someone or something.
LIT. To tell "mirabilia" about someone or something.

Fare mirabilia: To work wonders.
LIT. To do "mirabilia."

MISERIA (LA) Poverty

Pianger miseria: To complain of (and exaggerate) one's misfortunes, to plead poverty.
LIT. To cry poverty.

> *Piange sempre miseria* e poi ecco che il suo bravo viaggetto a Natale se lo fa ogni anno anche lui! (He's always telling you how terribly hard up he is, yet, come Christmas, off he goes to Florida for his little fling!)

MOCCOLO (IL) Candle bit

Accendere un moccolo: To thank one's lucky stars; to be grateful for a narrow escape.
LIT. To light a candle bit.

Tirare moccoli: To swear.
LIT. To throw candle bits.

MODA (LA) Fashion

Di moda: Fashionable; in fashion.
LIT. Of fashion.

> Va *molto di moda.* (It's *the* thing.)

MOGLIE (LA) Wife

Essere la moglie di Cesare*: Said of people or institutions which cannot afford to have even the slightest hint of suspicion cast upon them.
LIT. To be Caesar's wife.

---

* A reference to Caesar's words in repudiation of his wife Pompea.

Moglie e buoi dei paesi tuoi: Stick to your own people (when choosing a mate).

LIT. Wife and oxen from your own country.

Tra moglie e marito non mettere il dito (See **Dito**)

Voler la botte piena e la moglie ubriaca (See also **Bere e zufolare**): To want to have one's cake and eat it too.

LIT. To want the cask full and the wife drunk.

Voler la botte piena e la moglie *umbriaca*

MONDO (IL) World

Caschi il mondo: Come hell or high water.

LIT. Let the world fall.

> Io, domani mattina—*caschi il mondo*—voglio andare a trovarlo. (Tomorrow morning—come hell or high water—I'm going to go see him.)

Cose dell'altro mondo: Unheard of!

LIT. Things of the other world.

Così va il mondo: C'est la vie; that's the way the cookie crumbles.
LIT. Thus goes the world.

Da che mondo è mondo: From time immemorial; since the beginning of time.
LIT. Since the world is the world.

Ma, caro mio, *da che mondo è mondo* si sa che queste cose si fanno per iscritto! (But, my dear, everyone knows that this kind of thing has to be settled in writing!)

Il mondo è fatto a scale, chi le scende e chi le sale: Some people have all the luck! The rich get richer and the poor get poorer.
LIT. The world is made of stairs, some people descend them and some climb them.

Mandare qualcuno all'altro mondo: To send someone to kingdom come.
LIT. To send someone to the other world.

Mezzo mondo: Everybody and his brother.
LIT. Half the world.

Tutto il mondo è paese (See **Paese**)

MONETA (LA) Coin

Pagare di egual moneta, ripagare di egual moneta: To pay someone back in kind.
LIT. To pay someone back in his own coin.

Prendere qualcosa per moneta buona (See also **prender per Oro colato**): To take something at face value.
LIT. To take something for good coin.

MONTE (IL) Mountain

Andare a monte (See also **andare all'Aria**): To be called off.
LIT. To go to the mountain.

Mandare a monte qualcosa (See also **mandare all'Aria**): To call something off.
LIT. To send something to the mountain.

Promettere mari e monti (See **Mare**)

Smuovere mare e monti (See **Mare**)

MORTE (LA) Death

Altro è parlar di morte, altro è morire: It's one thing to speak of death and another to die.

Avercela a morte con qualcuno (See **Avere**)

È la sua morte: It hits the spot! Just perfect (used especially in connection with food).
LIT. It is its death.

> Questo pesce è squisito. E col vino bianco! *È la sua morte!* (This fish is wonderful. And with white wine! Just as it should be.)

La morte ci ha da trovar vivi: Death must find us alive.

Prendersela per il boccon della morte (See **Boccone**)

MORTO Dead

Essere più morto che vivo: To be quite shaken with fright.
LIT. To be more dead than alive.

Morto di fame: Abjectly poor; also, good for nothing, failure.
LIT. Dead of hunger.

Natura morta: Still life.
LIT. Dead nature.

MOSCA (LA) Fly

Far d'una mosca un elefante: To make a mountain out of a molehill.
LIT. To make an elephant of a fly.

Far la mosca cocchiera: To act as if the whole show was one's doing.
LIT. To play the coachman fly.

Far saltar la mosca al naso: To irritate to the point of distraction; to get someone's goat.
LIT. To make the fly jump at the nose.

Ha l'arte di *farmi saltar la mosca al naso.* (He really has a way of bugging me.)

Mosca bianca: Great exception; rara avis.
LIT. White fly.

Raro come *le mosche bianche.* (Scarce as hen's teeth.)

Mosca cieca: Blindman's buff.
LIT. Blind fly.

Mosca (See also **Acqua in bocca!**): Mum's the word!
LIT. Fly.

Non si sentiva volare una mosca: You could have heard a pin drop.
LIT. One didn't hear a fly flying.

Prender un fucile per acchiappare una mosca: To make a big production out of an ordinary occurrence.
LIT. To take a rifle in order to catch a fly.

Fargli parlar da un avvocato? Che esagerazione! *Un fucile per acchiappar una mosca!* (You're going to have your lawyer call him? I don't think you need all that heavy artillery!)

Rimanere con un pugno di mosche: To be left empty-handed; to be thwarted in one's scheming.
LIT. To remain with a handful of flies.

Gli sta bene! Voleva papparsi tutto lui, ed *è rimasto con un pugno di mosche.* (It serves him right! He wanted to grab it all for himself, and he ended up with nothing.)

Si prendono più mosche con una goccia di miele che con un barile d'aceto: You can catch more flies with a drop of honey than with a barrel of vinegar.

MOTUS (Latin for) Motion, movement

Motu proprio: By one's own initiative.

Dì la verità, l'ha fatto *motu proprio* o sei stato tu a suggerirglielo? (Tell the truth, was this his idea or were you the one to suggest it?)

MULINO (IL) Mill

Combattere con i mulini a vento: To tilt at windmills; to fight an imaginary foe.
LIT. To fight with windmills.

Parlare come un mulino a vento: To talk uninterruptedly, like a mill race; to be a chatterbox.
LIT. To talk like a windmill.

Tirar l'acqua al proprio mulino (See **Acqua**)

MURO (IL) Wall

Battere la testa contro un muro: To beat one's head against a stone wall.

Essere tra l'uscio e il muro (See **Uscio**)

Parlare al muro: To talk to a stone wall.
LIT. To talk to the wall.

MUSO (IL) Snout

Allungare il muso: To pull a long face.
LIT. To lengthen one's snout.

A muso duro: Resolutely; without fear.
LIT. With hard snout.

Mettere il muso: To sulk.
LIT. To put the snout.

È inutile che *tu mi metta il muso,* sai bene che ho ragione. (There's no point in sulking, you know perfectly well that I'm right.)

NASO (IL) Nose

A lume di naso: Taking a rough guess.
LIT. By light of nose.

> *A lume di naso,* direi un trentina di chilometri. (Off the top of my head, I'd say thirty kilometers.)

Arricciare il naso: To turn up one's nose.
LIT. To curl up one's nose.

Avere buon naso: To be intuitively correct in one's judgment; to have a good sense of smell.
LIT. To have good nose.

> Che t'avevo detto? È inutile, in certe cose *ho proprio buon naso!* (What did I tell you? You'll have to admit I have a feeling about some things!)

Avere la puzza al naso: To look down on everybody; to be a snob.
LIT. To have the foul smell at one's nose.

> Non so perché te la prendi. Tutti sanno che è uno con *la puzza al naso!* (I don't know why you're taking it so hard. Everyone knows he's a hopeless snob!)

Far saltar la mosca al naso (See **Mosca**)

Ficcare il naso negli affari altrui: To stick one's nose in other people's business.

Ficcanaso: Busybody.

Menare per il naso: To lead someone around by the nose; to have someone wound around one's little finger.

Non veder più in là del proprio naso: Not to see any further than (the end of) one's nose.

Non ricordarsi dal naso alla bocca (See **Bocca**)

Menare per il naso

Restare con un palmo di naso: To be thwarted in one's evil or mischievous intentions.
LIT. To remain with a nose a palm long.

> Credeva che ci cascassi ed *è rimasto con un palmo di naso!* (He thought I'd fall for it. You should have seen his face!)

NEGARE To deny

Essere negato per qualcosa: To have no talent for something.
LIT. To be denied for something.

NERO Black

Essere nero: To be in a black mood; to be gloomy.
LIT. To be black.

Far vedere bianco per nero: To pass off one thing for another.
LIT. To show white for black.

Se uno ti desse retta, con le tue chiacchiere saresti capace di *fargli vedere bianco per nero.* (If a person listened to you, with all your talk, you'd have him believing that black is white.)

Mettere nero su bianco: To put something down in black and white.
LIT. To put black on white.

NERVO (IL) Nerve

Avere i nervi: To be irritable.
LIT. To have the nerves.

Lasciami in pace, che oggi *ho i nervi!* (Please leave me alone. I'm not in the mood today!)

Dare su i nervi a qualcuno: To get on someone's nerves.
LIT. To give on the nerves to someone.

NIENTE Nothing

Non farne di niente: To give up the idea.
LIT. To do nothing of it.

Credo sia meglio *non farne di niente.* (I think it's best to forget about it.)

NOTTE (LA) Night

Una notte bianca: A totally sleepless night.
LIT. A white night.

NOZZE (LE) Wedding

Andare a nozze: To be delighted about something.
LIT. To go to a wedding.

Quando posso sentire un po' di buona musica, *io vado a nozze.* (When I can listen to some good music, I'm on top of the world.)

Andare a nozze

Far le nozze coi fichi secchi: To attempt to do something with inadequate means, to be close-fisted on an important occasion.
LIT. To do the wedding with dried figs.

Un cocktail di cinquanta persone con quella somma? Sei pazza, tu vorresti *far le nozze coi fichi secchi!* (A cocktail party for fifty people for that little money? You're crazy! If you're going to do it at all, you'll have to do it right.)

Invitare qualcuno a nozze (See also **invitare la Lepre a correre**): To ask someone to do something he is especially eager or well-equipped to do.
LIT. To invite someone to a wedding.

Portare la tua macchina in città? *M'inviti a nozze!* (Drive your car into the city? There's nothing I'd rather do!)

NUDO Naked

Nudo madre, nudo come Dio l'ha fatto, nudo come un verme: Stark naked; in one's birthday suit; without a stitch on.
LIT. Mother naked; naked as God made him; naked as a worm.

Verità nuda e cruda: The plain unvarnished truth.
LIT. Naked and raw truth.

NUOVO New

Nuovo fiammante, nuovo di zecca: Brand new.
LIT. Flaming new; new from the mint.

NUVOLA (LA) Cloud

Aver la testa nelle nuvole: To have one's head in the clouds.

Cadere dalle nuvole: To be dumfounded.
LIT. To fall from the clouds.

Quando gli ho parlato del concerto, *è caduto dalle nuvole.* (When I mentioned the concert to him, he said that was the first he'd heard of it.)

Aver la testa nelle nuvole

O

OCA (L') Goose

Avere un cervello d'oca: To be a bird brain.
LIT. To have the brain of a goose.

Esser figlio dell'oca bianca: To be great; to be entitled to special treatment.
LIT. To be the white goose's son.

> Cosa crede, *d'esser figlio dell'oca bianca?* (Does he think he's some kind of privileged person?)

Pelle d'oca: Goose flesh.
LIT. Goose skin.

OCCHIO (L') Eye

A colpo d'occhio: At a glance.

LIT. At blow of eye.

Ho capito *a colpo d'occhio* che non valeva la pena di restarci. (The minute we got there, I could see there was no point in staying.)

A occhi chiusi: Trustingly; with one's eyes closed.
LIT. At eyes closed.

A occhio e croce (See **Croce**)

A occhio nudo: To the naked eye.

A quattr'occhi: In private; in tête-à-tête.
LIT. At four eyes.

L'ho preso *a quattr'occhi.* (I took him aside.)

A perdita d'occhio: As far as the eye can see.
LIT. At loss of eye.

Aprire gli occhi a qualcuno: To open someone's eyes.

Aver qualcuno come il fumo agli occhi (See **Fumo**)

A vista d'occhio: Under one's very eyes; visibly.
LIT. At sight of eye.

Questo ragazzo cresce *a vista d'occhio.* (This boy is really growing by leaps and bounds.)

Chiudere un occhio: To look the other way.
LIT. To close an eye.

Costare un occhio della testa: To be very expensive; to cost an arm and a leg.
LIT. To cost an eye of one's head.

Dare nell'occhio: To be conspicuous, showy.
LIT. To give in the eye.

Quella cravatta *dà un po' nell'occhio.* (That tie is a bit too loud.) Usciamo dalla porta di dietro, così *non diamo troppo nell'occhio.* (Let's leave by the back door, so we won't attract so much attention.)

Dare un occhio per: To give one's eyetooth for.
LIT. To give an eye for.

Dormire ad occhi aperti: To be asleep on one's feet.
LIT. To sleep at open eyes.

Dormire con gli occhi aperti: To sleep with one eye open.
LIT. To sleep with open eyes.

Dormire con un occhio solo: To sleep with one eye open.
LIT. To sleep with only one eye.

Essere la pupilla degli occhi di qualcuno: To be the apple of someone's eye.
LIT. To be the pupil of someone's eye.

Fare gli occhiacci a qualcuno, dare un'occhiataccia a qualcuno: To give someone a dirty look.
LIT. To make the big bad eyes at someone; to give a bad look to someone.

> Come, non ti sei accorto che era arrabbiata? Non hai visto *l'occhiataccia che mi ha dato?* (What do you mean, you didn't notice she was mad? Didn't you see the way she looked at me?)

Fare gli occhi dolci a qualcuno: To make cow eyes at someone.
LIT. To make the sweet eyes at someone.

Far l'occhio di triglia: To make sheep's eyes at someone.
LIT. To make the mullet's eye.

Far l'occhiolino a qualcuno: To make eyes at someone; to wink at someone.
LIT. To make the little eye at someone.

Gettar la polvere negli occhi (See **Polvere**)

Guardare con la coda dell'occhio (See **Coda**)

In un batter d'occhio: In the twinkling of an eye.
LIT. In the beating of an eye.

> Per fortuna è arrivato X e ha messo tutto a posto *in un batter d'occhio.* (Fortunately, X came in and straightened everything out in no time.)

L'occhio del padrone ingrassa il cavallo: Nothing makes business prosper like the owner's personal attention.
LIT. The eye of the master fattens the horse.

Lontan dagli occhi lontan dal cuore: Out of sight, out of mind.
LIT. Far from the eyes far from the heart.

Non chiudere occhio: Not to sleep a wink.
LIT. Not to close an eye.

Non vedere che per gli occhi di qualcuno: To be blindly devoted to someone.
LIT. To see only through someone's eyes.

> *Non vede che per gli occhi* di quel bambino. (He's completely crazy about that child.)

Occhio che non vede cuore che non duole: What you don't know won't hurt you.
LIT. Eye that doesn't see heart that doesn't ache.

Perdere il lume degli occhi (See **Lume**)

Pugno in un occhio: Something shocking to the eye; in bad taste; garish.
LIT. Blow in the eye.

> Quella camicia è *un pugno in un occhio.* (That shirt sticks out like a sore thumb.)

Saltare agli occhi: To be obvious; to hit in the eye.
LIT. To jump to the eyes.

> Non te ne sei accorto? Ma *salta agli occhi!* (How could you have missed it? It's as plain as the nose on your face!)

Sognare ad occhi aperti: To be seeing things; to indulge in wishful thinking.
LIT. To dream with open eyes.

> Figurati se lui si scomoda per aiutare un amico. *Sogni ad occhi aperti!* (You're living in a dream world if you think he'd go out of his way for a friend!)

Strizzar l'occhio: To wink.
LIT. To squeeze the eye.

Tener d'occhio qualcuno: To keep an eye on someone.
LIT. To keep someone of eye.

Un pruno in un occhio (See also **Spina nel fianco**): A thorn in one's side.
LIT. A thorn in an eye.

Vedere di buon occhio: To be well-disposed toward; to look kindly upon.
LIT. To see of good eye.

> Non credo· *veda di buon occhio* l'idea che sua figlia sposi un attore. (I don't think he's so keen about the idea of his daughter marrying an actor.)

OLIO (L') Oil

Andar liscio come l'olio: To work out beautifully; to go as smooth as silk.
LIT. To go as smooth as oil.

Buttare olio sul fuoco (See **Fuoco**)

Zitto come l'olio: Quiet as a mouse.
LIT. Silent like oil.

OMBRA (L') Shade, shadow

Aver paura della propria ombra: To be afraid of one's own shadow.

Correre dietro alle ombre: To go on a wild-goose chase; to be deceived by appearances.
LIT. To run after shadows.

Dar corpo alle ombre: To voice hidden fears; to give importance to trifling matters.
LIT. To give body to shades.

> Non vorrei *dar corpo alle ombre*, ma mi pare che non vadano più d'accordo come una volta. (I don't want to make

too much out of it, but I have a feeling that they don't get along the way they used to.)

Dar ombra: To give offense to; to arouse suspicion.
LIT. To give shade.

Basta una parola a *dargli ombra.* (Even a word is enough to hurt him.)

Nemmeno per ombra (See also **nemmeno per Sogno**): Not in the least; I wouldn't dream of it.
LIT. Not even for shade.

ONORE (L') Honor

A onor del vero: To be fair about it; to give credit where credit is due.
LIT. In honor of truth.

Fare gli onori: To do the honors.

Per onor di firma: In order to live up to a commitment.
LIT. For honor of signature.

A dirti la verità, ne avrei abbastanza. Se continuo, è solo *per onor di firma.* (To tell you the truth, I've really had enough. I only go on because I feel obligated to see the thing through.)

ORA (L') Hour

Alla buon'ora: Glad to hear it! At last! Good for you!
LIT. In the good hour.

L'hai licenziato? *Alla buon'ora!* (You fired him? That's a piece of good news!)

Era ora: It was high time!
LIT. It was hour.

Fare le ore piccole: To stay up until the wee hours.
LIT. To make the small hours.

Far ora: To pass the time until a given hour.
LIT. To do hour.

Se vuoi, posso accompagnarti. Ho un appuntamento alle cinque e mi servirà per *far ora*. (If you like, I'll come with you. I have an hour to kill until my five o'clock appointment anyway.)

Non veder l'ora di: To look forward to.
LIT. Not to see the hour of.

Non vedo l'ora che arrivi l'estate. (I can't wait till summer comes.)

Ora bruciata: In the heat of the day.
LIT. Burned hour.

Non uscirei a queste *ore bruciate* per tutto l'oro del mondo. (I wouldn't go out at this time of the day if you gave me a million dollars.)

Ora di punta: Rush hour.
LIT. Edge hour.

Ora morta: Slack time.
LIT. Dead hour.

ORECCHIO (L') Ear

Ascoltare da un orecchio solo: To pay little attention to what is being said.
LIT. To listen with only one ear.

Per dirglielo, gliel'ho detto, ma mi è parso *ascoltasse da un orecchio solo*. (I did tell him, I assure you, but it didn't look to me as if he had his mind on what I was saying.)

Dare una tiratina d'orecchi a qualcuno: To scold someone in a mild, fatherly way.
LIT. To give someone a little ear-pulling.

Entrare da un orecchio e uscire dall'altro: To go in one ear and out the other.

Fare orecchi da mercante (See **Fare**)

Mettere una pulce nell'orecchio a qualcuno: To put a bug, a flea, in someone's ear.

Non sentirci da quell'orecchio: To be deaf to all arguments on a given subject.
LIT. Not to hear from that ear.

È inutile parlargli di studio. Lui *da quell'orecchio non ci sente.* (It's no use trying to talk to him about studying. As far as that subject is concerned, your arguments will fall on deaf ears.)

Rizzare le orecchie: To prick up one's ears.
LIT. To raise one's ears.

ORMA (L') Footprint.

Seguire le orme di: To follow in someone's footsteps.
LIT. To follow someone's footprints.

ORO (L') Gold

Non è tutt'oro quel che luccica: All that glitters is not gold.

Non per tutto l'oro del mondo: Not for all the tea in China.
LIT. Not for all the gold in the world.

Nuotare nell'oro: To be rolling in money.
LIT. To swim in gold.

Prender per oro colato (See also **prendere qualcosa per Moneta buona**): To take something at face value.
LIT. To take for molten gold.

Sei troppo ingenuo, figlio mio! *Prendi* tutto quel che la gente dice *per oro colato!* (You're too naive, my boy! You accept everything people tell you as if it were the Gospel truth!)

Valere tant'oro quanto si pesa: To be worth one's weight in gold.
LIT. To be worth as much gold as one weighs.

OSPITE (L') Guest, host

Andarsene insalutato ospite: To leave without saying goodbye.
LIT. To leave (as) an ungreeted guest.

L'ospite è come il pesce, dopo tre giorni puzza: Facetious warning against wearing out one's welcome.
LIT. A guest is like fish, after three days it stinks.

OSTE (L') Innkeeper

Domandare all'oste se il vino è buono: To ask an opinion of someone who is bound to be biased.
LIT. To ask the innkeeper if the wine is good.

Fare i conti senza l'oste: To leave some very important person or factor out of one's calculations; to reckon without one's host.
LIT. To add up the bill without the innkeeper.

> No, non è più andato. *Aveva fatto i conti senza l'oste* e fatto assegnamento sull'automobile di X! (No, he didn't go after all. He forgot to consult one very important person —X, whose car he was going to take!)

OVATTA (L') Cotton wool

Tenere qualcuno nell'ovatta: To keep someone wrapped in cotton wool.

OZIO (L') Idleness

L'ozio è il padre dei vizi: The devil finds mischief for idle hands to do.
LIT. Idleness is the father of vices.

P

PACE (LA) Peace

Darsi pace: To become reconciled to a difficult situation.
LIT. To give oneself peace.

Che quel ragazzo abbia lasciato gli studi . . . *non me ne posso dar pace!* (The one thing I can't resign myself to is that a boy like him has left college.)

PADELLA (LA) Frying pan

Avere un occhio alla gatta e uno alla padella (See **Gatto**)

Cadere dalla padella nella brace: To fall out of the frying pan into the fire.
LIT. To fall from the frying pan into the embers.

PADRONE (IL) Master, owner

Padrone! Padronissimo: Suit yourself! It's your funeral!
LIT. Master! Very much the master!

Padronissimo! Ma te ne pentirai! (You're the doctor! But you'll be sorry!)

L'occhio del padrone ingrassa il cavallo (See **Occhio**)

PAESE (IL) Country, town, village

Paese che vai usanza che trovi: When in Rome, do as the Romans do.
LIT. Country that you go, custom that you find.

Tutto il mondo è paese: People are the same everywhere.
LIT. The whole world is a village.

PAGARE To pay

Pagare di persona: To be personally liable; to give generously of oneself.
LIT. To pay of person.

È un uomo con cui si lavora bene, perché è sempre disposto a *pagare di persona.* (He's a good person to work with because he's not asking you to do anything he's not willing to do himself.)

Pagare profumatamente: To pay through the nose.
LIT. To pay fragrantly.

Pagare salato: To pay an extravagant price.
LIT. To pay salted.

A pagare e morire c'è sempre tempo: There's always plenty of time for paying and dying.

PAGLIA (LA) Straw

Aver la coda di paglia: To be on the defensive because of an uneasy conscience.
LIT. To have a tail of straw.

Aver la coda di paglia

Quando ha parlato di lettere di ringraziamento, mi sono sentito *la coda di paglia*. Non sono affatto sicuro di avergliene mai mandata una! (When she mentioned thank-you notes, I didn't know where to look. I'm not at all sure I ever sent her one.)

Col tempo e con la paglia: That's what you think! Fat chance!
LIT. With time and with straw.

"Vedrai, col tempo tutto si accomoderà." "Sì, *col tempo e con la paglia. . . !*" ("You'll see, in time it will all work out." "That's what you say!")

Essere sulla paglia: To be completely destitute; to be down to one's last cent.
LIT. To be on the straw.

Fuoco di paglia: Flash in the pan.
LIT. Fire of straw.

Inciampare in un filo di paglia: To fail on account of a trifle.
LIT. To trip on a straw.

Mettere la paglia accanto al fuoco (See **Fuoco**)

Uomo di paglia: Straw man

PALLA (LA) Ball

Avere il pallino di: To be nuts on the subject of.

LIT. To have the little ball of.

In questo periodo *ha il pallino* della caccia e nei weekend non ci si ragiona. (At this time of year, he's on a hunting kick and there's no talking to him on weekends.)

Cogliere la palla al balzo: To jump at the chance.
LIT. To catch the ball on the rebound.

Parlava dell'alto costo della vita, e io *ho colto la palla al balzo* e gli ho fatto capire che avevo bisogno di un aumento. (He was talking about the high cost of living, so I seized the opportunity to let him know that I needed a raise.)

Essere un pallone gonfiato: To be pompous; conceited; full of hot air.
LIT. To be a blown-up balloon.

PALMA (LA) Palm

Dare la palma a qualcuno: To give the prize to.
LIT. To give the palm to someone.

In fatto di cucina, bisogna *darti la palma.* (When it comes to cooking, you're really tops.)

Ottenere la palma, riportare la palma: To take the palm; to carry off the prize.

PALMENTO (IL) Millstone

Mangiare a quattro palmenti: To eat heartily.
LIT. To eat by four millstones.

Dare la palma

PALO (IL) Pole

Fare il palo: To be the lookout while a robbery is being performed.
LIT. To do the pole.

Saltare di palo in frasca: To jump from one subject to another.
LIT. To jump from pole to branch.

> Saltando di *palo in frasca,* che ne è di X? (A propos of nothing, whatever happened to X?)

PANCA (LA) Bench

Scaldare le panche: To work or study without profit; to sit like a bump on a log.
LIT. To warm the benches.

> O studiate o ve ne andate. Non state qui a *scaldar le panche!* (Either get down to work or get out. You're not here for your health!)

PANCIA (LA) Stomach, belly

Tenersi la pancia dal ridere: To be in stitches; to split one's sides from laughter.
LIT. To hold one's stomach out of laughing.

PANCIOLLE (Used only in the following context)

Stare in panciolle: To laze around.
LIT. To be in "panciolle."

PANE (IL) Bread

Buono come il pane: As good as gold.
LIT. Good like bread.

Chi ha il pane non ha i denti (e chi ha i denti non ha il pane): He who has the opportunity lacks the ability, and vice versa.
LIT. He who has the bread has not the teeth. . . .

Dare il pane e la sassata: To do someone a favor and be unpleasant about it.
LIT. To give the bread and the stoning.

> C'era da aspettarselo. Non è capace di *dare il pane senza la sassata.* (I might have known. Whenever she does something for you, she makes you pay dearly for it.)

Dir pane al pane: To call a spade a spade.
LIT. To say bread to the bread.

Essere pane e cacio (See **Cacio**)

Mangiare il pane a ufo, mangiare il pane a tradimento: Not to earn one's keep.
LIT. To eat bread without paying; to eat bread treacherously.

Mangiare pan pentito: To eat humble pie.
LIT. To eat sorry bread.

Per un boccon di pane (See **Boccone**)

Render pan per focaccia: To give tit for tat; to give as good as one gets.
LIT. To give back bread for pie.

Se non è zuppa è pan bagnato: Six of one and half a dozen of the other.
LIT. If it's not soup it's wet bread.

Togliersi il pane di bocca: To make all sorts of sacrifices; to go without the bare necessities.
LIT. To take the bread out of one's own mouth.

> E pensare che in quegli anni *mi son tolto il pane di bocca* perché non le mancasse nulla! (And to think that during those years I denied myself everything so that she wouldn't want for anything.)

Trovare pane per i propri denti: To meet one's match.
LIT. To find bread for one's teeth.

PANNO (IL) Cloth

Dio manda il freddo secondo i panni (See **Dio**)

I panni sporchi si lavano in casa: Dirty linen should be washed at home.

Mettersi nei panni di qualcuno: To put oneself in someone else's shoes.

Tagliare i panni *addosso*

LIT. To put oneself in someone's clothes.

Tagliare i panni addosso a qualcuno: To rake someone over the coals.
LIT. To cut the clothes on someone's back.

Preferisco andar a vedere un buon film piuttosto che passar la serata a *tagliar i panni addosso* alla gente. (I'd rather take in a good movie than sit around all evening taking other people apart.)

PAPA (IL) Pope

Andare a Roma e non vedere il papa: To overlook the most important feature of something.
LIT. To go to Rome and not see the Pope.

Da Zì Teresa e non avete ordinato pesce? È come *andare a Roma e non vedere il papa!* (You went to Zì Teresa's restaurant and didn't have fish? Well, then you might just as well have stayed home!)

Morto un papa se ne fa un altro: No one is irreplaceable.
LIT. When a Pope is dead another is made.

Stare come un papa: To be at the height of comfort; to live like a king.
LIT. To be like a Pope.

Una volta ogni morte di papa: Once in a blue moon.
LIT. Once every Pope's death.

PAPPA (LA) Soup, porridge

Mangiar la pappa in capo a qualcuno: To be taller or smarter than someone else.
LIT. To eat the soup on someone's head.

Se non studi di più, il tuo fratellino finirà per *mangiarti la pappa in capo.* (If you don't work harder, your little brother will really show you up.)

Trovare la pappa fatta, trovare la pappa scodellata: To have everything handed to one on a silver platter.

LIT. To find the porridge made; to find the porridge dished out.

PARADISO (**IL**) Paradise, heaven

Voler andare in paradiso a dispetto dei santi: To insist on going where one is not welcome.
LIT. To want to go to paradise against the will of the saints.

Voler andare in paradiso in carrozza: To want credit for very little effort.
LIT. To want to go to Paradise in a cab.

Caro mio, una serata almeno per preparare l'articolo bisogna sacrificarla. Tu *vorresti andare in paradiso in carrozza!* (You'll have to devote at least one evening to writing that article. You can't expect to get something for nothing!)

Voler andare in paradiso *in carrozza*

PARI Even

Essere pari e patta: To be quits.
LIT. To be even and tied.

PARLARE To speak

Parlare a nuora perché suocera intenda: To refer to a difficulty or complaint indirectly.

LIT. To speak to the daughter-in-law so that the mother-in-law understands.

Hai sentito i suoi commenti sul matrimonio? Son sicuro *che parlava a nuora* . . . (Did you hear his comments on marriage? I'm sure they were intended for our benefit.)

Parlare a torto e traverso: To talk through one's hat.
LIT. To speak wrongly and crookedly.

Parlare a vanvera: To talk off the top of one's head.
LIT. To speak at "vanvera" (used only in this connection).

Parlare del più e del meno: To talk of nothing in particular, of this and that.
LIT. To talk of the most and the least.

Parlare grasso: To use gross language; to tell off-color jokes.
LIT. To talk fat.

Parlare in punta di forchetta (See **Forchetta**)

Parlare per dar fiato alla bocca: To talk nonsense; to speak just to hear oneself talk.
LIT. To speak in order to give breath to the mouth.

Non te la prendere, lo sai che *parla per dar fiato alla bocca!* (Don't pay any attention to him, you know he's in love with the sound of his own voice!)

PAROLA (LA) Word

A buon intenditor poche parole: A word to the wise is sufficient.
LIT. To someone who understands well, few words.

A parole: To hear him talk; on paper.
LIT. In words.

A parole, sembra un lavoro da nulla. Sapessi invece il tempo che mi ha preso! (Theoretically, the job seems a cinch. You should see how much time was involved!) *A parole,* non c'è sacrificio che non farebbe per quella figlia. (To hear him talk, there's nothing he wouldn't do for that daughter of his.)

Avere la parola facile: To be articulate.
LIT. To have the word easy.

> Beato te che *hai la parola facile.* (I'd give anything to be as articulate as you are.)

Domandare la parola: To ask leave to speak; to ask for the floor.
LIT. To ask for the word.

È una parola: Easier said than done!
LIT. It's a word.

In parole povere: In plain words.
LIT. In poor words.

> *In parole povere,* sei stufo? (In plain words, you've had enough?)

Mancare di parola: To fail to keep one's word.
LIT. To lack of word.

Mettere le parole in bocca a qualcuno: To put words in someone's mouth.

Mettere una buona parola per: To put in a good word for.

Passare dalle parole ai fatti: To go from words to blows.
LIT. To pass from words to deeds.

> Non c'è voluto molto perché *passassero dalle parole ai fatti.* (It didn't take them long to come to blows.)

Prendere la parola: To take the floor.
LIT. To take the word.

Prendere qualcuno in parola: To take someone at his word.
LIT. To take someone in word.

Rimangiarsi la parola: To go back on one's word.
LIT. To re-eat the word.

> Mi dispiace moltissimo, ma purtroppo sono costretto a *rimangiarmi la parola.* (I'm really terribly sorry, but I'm forced to renege on my promise.)

Rubare le parole di bocca a qualcuno: To take the words out of someone's mouth.

LIT. To steal the words from someone's mouth.

PARS (Latin for) Part

Essere magna pars: To be very influential.
LIT. To be great part.

> Perché non ne parli a X? Mi dicono che *è magna pars* nell'assunzione del personale. (Why don't you talk to X about it? I hear he's got a lot to say about the hiring of personnel.)

PARTITO (**IL**) Resolution, condition, political party

Mettere la testa a partito: To settle down; to turn over a new leaf.
LIT. To put one's head to resolution.

> Se davvero vuoi metter su famiglia, bisogna tu ti decida a *metter la testa a partito.* (If you're serious about getting married, you'll have to make up your mind to settle down.)

Per partito preso: Out of prejudice.
LIT. For resolution taken.

> Se gli dai torto anche in questa occasione, lo fai proprio *per partito preso.* (If you say he's wrong this time, too, then you must be prejudiced.)

Ridursi a mal partito: To be in a bad state.
LIT. To come to a bad condition.

PASSARE To pass

Passare il Rubicone: To take an irrevocable step; to cross the Rubicon.

PASSO (**IL**) Step

A due passi: A few steps away; around the corner; close by.
LIT. At two steps.

Fare due passi, fare quattro passi: To go for a short walk.
LIT. To make two steps, to make four steps.

Il tempo è così bello, perché *non facciamo due passi?* (It's such a beautiful day, why don't we take a walk around the block?)

Fare il passo più lungo della gamba (See **Gamba**)

Far passi da gigante: To make extraordinary headway, giant strides.
LIT. To make steps worthy of a giant.

Far tre passi per ogni mattone: To walk at a snail's pace.
LIT. To make three steps for each brick.

Passo falso: False step, rash act; wrong move.

Ho paura che il comunicargli la nostra mancanza di contanti sia stato *un passo falso.* (I'm afraid that letting him know that we're short of cash was a big mistake.)

PASTA (LA) Dough, pie, pastry, noodles

Aver le mani in molte paste: To have a finger in every pie.

Aver le mani in pasta: To be in the midst of doing something.
LIT. To have one's hands in dough.

Ormai *ho le mani in pasta* . . . tanto vale che finisca io. (Now that I've started the job, I might as well finish.)

Essere una buona pasta (See also **buon Diavolo**): To be a good egg.
LIT. To be a good dough.

Uomo di pasta frolla: Morally weak man.
LIT. Man made of pastry.

Aver le mani in pasta

PATERNALE (LA) Reprimand, lecture

Fare una paternale a qualcuno: To talk to someone like a Dutch uncle.
LIT. To do the lecture to someone.

PAURA (LA) Fear

Meglio aver paura che buscarne: Better to be safe than sorry.
LIT. Better to be afraid than to get hit.

PAZZO Crazy

Cose da pazzi! Roba da pazzi: Never heard of such a thing!
LIT. Things worthy of lunatics.

PELLE (LA) Skin

Amici per la pelle (See **Amico**)

Aver la pelle dura: To be thick-skinned.
LIT. To have a hard skin.

Aver le lacrime in pelle in pelle (See **Lacrima**)

Far la pelle a qualcuno: To kill someone; to do him in.
LIT. To make the skin to someone.

Non star nella pelle: To be beside oneself with joy.
LIT. Not to stay in one's skin.

Ridere a crepapelle: To laugh till one's sides split.
LIT. To laugh to the point of splitting one's skin.

Rimetterci la pelle: To lose one's life in the process.
LIT. To lose one's skin there.

Salvare la pelle: To save one's skin.

Vendere cara la pelle: To put up a brave fight; to sell one's life dearly.
LIT. To sell one's skin dear.

La situazione era disperata, ma decidemmo di *vender*

cara la pelle. (The situation was hopeless, but we decided to give them a run for their money.)

Vender la pelle dell'orso prima di averlo: To count one's chickens before they are hatched.
LIT. To sell the bear's skin before catching him.

PELO (IL) Hair

A bruciapelo: Point-blank.
LIT. At hair-burning.

Cercare il pelo *nell'uovo*

Cercare il pelo nell'uovo: To be a perfectionist to the point of absurdity.
LIT. To look for the hair in the egg.

Non te la prendere se il tuo concerto non lo entusiasma. Sai che *cerca sempre il pelo nell'uovo.* (Don't be too upset if he's not thrilled by your performance. You know he's always trying to find the fly in the ointment.)

Di primo pelo: Very young.
LIT. Of first hair.

Ormai non è più un giovane *di primo pelo.* (He's not exactly a spring chicken.)

Non aver peli sulla lingua: Not to mince words.
LIT. Not to have hairs on one's tongue.

Per un pelo: By a hair, almost, by the skin of one's teeth.
LIT. For a hair.

Abbiamo avuto un incidente d'automobile e *per un pelo* non siamo finiti in un burrone. (We had an accident and just missed ending up in a ravine by a hair.) *Per un pelo* non gli ho detto la verità. (I almost told him the truth.)

PENNA (LA) Pen, feather

Farsi bello con le penne del pavone (See **Bello**)

Lasciarci le penne: To come out of a situation very badly.
LIT. To leave one's feathers in it.

Lasciare nella penna, rimanere nella penna: Said of the omission of a word or a phrase in writing.
LIT. To leave in the pen; to remain in the pen.

PENNELLO (IL) Brush

Calzare a pennello: To fit like a glove.
LIT. To fit at brush.

> Quel soprannome gli calza *a pennello.* (That nickname suits him to a "T".)

PENSARE To think

Nemmeno a pensarci: Not on your life; not in a million years.
LIT. Not even to think of it.

> Lui prendersi una vacanza? *Nemmeno a pensarci!* (Him? Take a vacation? He wouldn't dream of it!)

Una ne fa cento ne pensa: Said of a child who always has some mischief up his sleeve, or of a dynamic and unpredictable person.
LIT. One he does, one hundred he thinks of.

PENSIERO (IL) Thought

Essere sopra pensiero: To be lost in thought.
LIT. To be over (the) thought.

Levarsi il pensiero: (See **Levare**)

Stare in pensiero: To worry.
LIT. To be in thought.

Ormai dovresti conoscerlo e non *stare in pensiero* ogni volta che è in ritardo. (You should be used to him by now and not worry every time he's ten minutes late.)

PENTOLA (LA) Pot, saucepan

Qualcosa bolle in pentola: Something is brewing, cooking.
LIT. Something is boiling in the pot.

PERDERE To lose

È meglio perderlo che trovarlo: Good riddance to bad rubbish! He's bad news!
LIT. It's better to lose him than to find him.

Non lo rimpiangere! *È meglio perderlo che trovarlo.* (Don't waste any tears over him. You're better off without him!)

Perdere il treno: To miss the boat.
LIT. To lose (miss) the train.

Perdere la bussola: To lose one's sense of discernment or self-control.
LIT. To lose the compass.

Quando ho sentito la notizia, *ho perso la bussola* e non so neppur io che cosa ho detto. (When I heard about it, I was so upset I don't know what I said.)

PESCARE To fish

Pescare nel torbido: To fish in troubled waters; to profit from a questionable deal.

Vattelapesca: (See also **indovinala Grillo**): Your guess is as good as mine!
LIT. Go and fish it.

PESCE (IL) Fish

Essere un pesce fuori d'acqua: To be a fish out of water.

Fare il pesce in barile: To be hard to pin down; to hedge; to be as slippery as an eel.

LIT. To do the fish in (the) barrel.

Non credo arriveremo mai a un contratto. Il pezzo più grosso *sta facendo il pesce in barile.* (I don't think we'll ever come to an agreement. The top man keeps dodging the main issue.)

Né carne né pesce: Neither fish nor fowl.
LIT. Neither meat nor fish.

Non sapere che pesci pigliare: To be at a loss, not to know where to turn.
LIT. Not to know which fish to take.

Sano come un pesce: Fit as a fiddle.
LIT. Healthy as a fish.

PESO (IL) Weight

Usare due pesi e due misure: To use a double standard.
LIT. To use two weights and two measures.

La verità è che qui *si usano due pesi e due misure,* e da me si richiede un lavoro cento volte maggiore che dagli altri. (The truth of the matter is that there's a double standard around here, and I'm expected to work a hundred times harder than anybody else.)

PESTE (LA) Plague

Dire peste e corna di qualcuno: To speak very disparagingly of someone.
LIT. To say plague and horns of someone.

Ne ha sempre detto peste, e ora sono inseparabili. (She has always said the most awful things about him, and, all of a sudden, they're inseparable.)

PETTINE (IL) Comb

Tutti i nodi vengono al pettine: One's deeds have to be accounted for sooner or later.
LIT. All knots come to the comb.

PEZZO (IL) Piece

Farsi a pezzi per qualcuno: To go through fire and water for someone.
LIT. To tear oneself to pieces for someone.

Pezzo grosso: Big shot; big wheel; V.I.P.
LIT. Big piece.

Un uomo tutto d'un pezzo: A man of sterling character.
LIT. A man all of one piece.

PIACERE (IL) Pleasure, favor

. . . ch'è un ,piacere
LIT. . . . that is a pleasure.

Piove *ch'è un piacere!* (Boy, is it coming down!) Mangia *ch'è un piacere.* (It does your heart good to see him eat.)

Ma fammi il piacere: Don't give me that line! Don't be silly! Come, come!
LIT. But do me the favor.

PIAGA (LA) Wound, sore

Il medico pietoso fa la piaga cancrenosa: Spare the rod and spoil the child.
LIT. The compassionate doctor makes the wound gangrenous.

Mettere il dito sulla piaga: To hit the nail on the head.
LIT. To put the finger on the sore.

PIANGERE To cry

Piangere come una vite tagliata: To cry one's heart out.
LIT. To cry like a cut vine.

PIANTA

Di sana pianta: Entirely; afresh; from scratch.
LIT. From healthy (whole) plant.

Mi dispiace, ma questo va rifatto *di sana pianta.* (I'm sorry, but you'll have to do this all over again.)

Inventato di sana pianta: Made up of whole cloth.
LIT. Invented from healthy (whole) plant.

Fare il pianto *greco*

PIANTO (IL) Cry

Fare il pianto greco: To complain repeatedly and abundantly.
LIT. To make the Greek weeping.

> Su via, non mi *fare il pianto greco.* (Come on now, quit whining.)

PIATTO (IL) Plate, dish

Passare il piatto: To pass the hat.
LIT. To pass the plate.

Piatto forte: Main course; main attraction or number in a performance.
LIT. Strong dish.

Sputar nel piatto in cui s'è mangiato: To bite the hand that feeds you.
LIT. To spit in the plate in which one has eaten.

PIAZZA (LA) Square, market

Andare in piazza: To be in the process of becoming bald.
LIT. To go into square.

> *Sta andando un po' in piazza,* ma è sempre un bell'uomo. (He's starting to lose his hair, but he's still very attractive.)

Far piazza pulita: To make a clean sweep.
LIT. To make clean square.

> Bisognerebbe *facesse piazza pulita* di tutti gli elementi corrotti . . . (If he could only get rid of all those shady characters . . .)

Mettere in piazza: To publicize intimate feelings or private matters.
LIT. To put into (the) square.

> Ti prego di *non mettere in piazza* gli affari miei. (Please don't go and tell the whole world the details of my private life.)

Per quel che fa la piazza: Compared to current standards.
LIT. For what the market does.

> Non è la segretaria più dinamica del mondo, ma *per quel che fa la piazza* . . . (She's not the most dynamic secretary in the world, but if you think what you get these days . . .)

PICCA (LA) Spike, spades (cards)

Contare quanto il fante di picche: To count for nothing.
LIT. To count as much as the jack of spades.

Rispondere picche: To give a flat "no" for an answer.
LIT. To answer spades.

PIEDE (IL) Foot

Andare coi piedi di piombo: To watch one's step; to proceed with extreme caution, especially in financial matters.
LIT. To go with feet of lead.

A ogni pié sospinto: Very often, on the slightest pretext.
LIT. At every foot put forward.

> Con la scusa di prendere in prestito questo o quel libro, veniva in casa nostra *a ogni pié sospinto*. (He always had some excuse, such as borrowing this or that book, to come up to our house every other minute.)

A piede libero: Out on bail.
LIT. On free foot.

Aver le ali ai piedi, mettere le ali ai piedi: To have wings on one's heels.
LIT. To have wings on one's feet; to put wings on one's feet.

Avere un piede nella fossa: To have one foot in the grave.

Cadere in piedi: To land on one's feet.

Darsi la zappa sui piedi

Darsi la zappa sui piedi: To defeat one's own purpose; to cook one's own goose.
LIT. To give the hoe on one's own feet.

Si è dato la zappa sui piedi. Domandare un giorno di permesso e poi lasciarsi scappare che il lavoro non è finito! (He has only himself to blame. Who would ask for the day off and then let it slip that the work wasn't done?)

Farsi mettere i piedi sul collo: To let someone walk all over you.
LIT. To let someone put his feet on your neck.

Fuori dai piedi: Clear out!
LIT. Out of one's feet.

Guardare qualcuno da capo a piedi: To look someone up and down.
LIT. To look at someone from head to feet.

Leccapiedi: Shameless flatterer.

Leccare i piedi a qualcuno (See also **lustrar le Scarpe**): To lick someone's boots.
LIT. To lick someone's feet.

Prender piede: To get a foothold; to become prevalent.
LIT. To take foot.

È un uso incorretto, ma che ormai *ha preso piede.* (It's incorrect usage, but I'm afraid it's here to stay!) Ti sei accorta che la moda delle parrucche *sta prendendo sempre più piede?* (Have you noticed that the wig craze really seems to have taken over?)

Puntar i piedi: To stand one's ground; to dig in one's heels; to put one's foot down.
LIT. To brace one's feet.

Mi hanno fatto un'ottima offerta, ma questa volta *ho puntato i piedi* e non mi son lasciato persuadere. (They made me an excellent offer, but this time I stuck to my guns and didn't let them talk me into anything.)

Ragionare coi piedi: To be illogical, sloppy in one's thinking.
LIT. To think with one's feet.

Ma questo, scusa, si chiama *ragionare coi piedi*. (Forgive me, but that's an argument worthy of a two-year-old.)

Su due piedi: Without warning; right then and there; on the spot.
LIT. On two feet.

Mi ha piantato *su due piedi*. (He left me cold.)

Vivere su un gran piede: To live luxuriously, in style.
LIT. To live on a large foot.

PIENO Full

In pieno: Completely, precisely; in full swing.
LIT. In full.

La sua osservazione l'ha colpito *in pieno*. (His criticism really struck home.) La stagione musicale è *in pieno*. (The musical season is in full swing.)

Pieno di sé: Conceited; egotistical; a stuffed shirt.
LIT. Full of oneself.

PIETRA (LA) Stone

La pietra per il proprio anello: The answer to one's prayers.
LIT. The stone for one's ring.

Mettere una pietra sopra a qualcosa: To forgive and forget; to let bygones be bygones.
LIT. To put a stone over something.

Mettiamoci una pietra sopra e non parliamone più. (Let's forget the whole thing; it's not worth arguing about.)

Pietra dello scandalo: Source of trouble.
LIT. The stone of the scandal.

Puoi star sicuro che *la pietra dello scandalo* è sempre lui. (You may be sure that when there's trouble he's behind it.)

Pietra di paragone: Basis for comparison; touchstone.
LIT. Stone for comparison.

Quello è un uomo eccezionale. Non puoi farne una *pietra di paragone*. (He's an exceptional person. You can't judge others by the same standards.)

PIFFERO (IL) Fife, piper

Come i pifferi di montagna (che andarono per suonare e furono suonati) (See also **andar per Lana**): To go for wool and come home shorn.
LIT. Like the mountain pipers (who went to play and were played instead).

PILLOLA (LA) Pill

Indorare la pillola: To try to make unpleasant events or news palatable, to sugarcoat the pill.
LIT. To gild the pill.

Ingoiare la pillola: To swallow a (bitter) pill.

PIOGGIA (LA) Rain

Far la pioggia e il bel tempo: To be boss, to call all the shots.
LIT. To make the rain and the fair weather.

Purtroppo, in questo campo sono i critici che *fanno la pioggia e il bel tempo*. (Unfortunately, in this business the critics can make or break you.)

PIOVERE To rain

Non ci piove né ci nevica: Said of an irrevocable decision.
LIT. It neither rains nor snows on it.

Quando mio padre ha detto una cosa, puoi esser sicuro
che non ci piove né ci nevica. (When my father decides on
something, you can be sure that's the way it's going to be.)

Piove sul bagnato: It never rains but it pours.
LIT. It rains on the wet.

PISOLINO (IL) Nap

Schiacciare un pisolino: To take a nap.
LIT. To crush a nap.

PIÙ More, most

A più non posso: With an all-out effort.
LIT. At more-I-cannot.

Abbiamo spinto *a più non posso,* ma la macchina non si
è mossa. (We pushed as hard as we could, but the car
didn't budge.)

Non plus ultra: The ultimate; the peak of; the limit.
LIT. (Latin for) Not any further.

Questo è il *non plus ultra!* (This beats them all!) E il *non
plus ultra* dell'arroganza! (I never heard of such inso-
lence!)

Non poterne più: Not to be able to stand something any
longer.
LIT. Not to be able of something any more.

Ho lavorato tutta la settimana come un facchino. *Non
ne posso più!* (I worked like a horse all week. I'm exhausted!) *Non ne posso più dalla fame.* (I'm so hungry I
can't stand it.)

Parlare del più e del meno (See **Parlare**)

POLLO (**IL**) Chicken

Alzarsi coi polli: To be an early riser; to get up with the birds.
LIT. To get up with the chickens.

Andar a letto coi polli: To go to bed with the chickens; to keep early hours.

Conoscere i propri polli: To know one's customers.
LIT. To know one's chickens.

Far ridere i polli: To be absurd, ridiculous.
LIT. To make the chickens laugh.

Ma va, non dire delle assurdità. *Far ridere i polli.* (Come on, don't be ridiculous. It's enough to make a horse laugh.)

Far ridere i polli

POLO (**IL**) Pole

Essere a due poli opposti: To be at (two) opposite poles; to be poles apart.

POLVERE (**LA**) Dust, powder

Gettar la polvere negli occhi a qualcuno: To throw dust in someone's eyes.

Mordere la polvere: To bite the dust.

Non ha inventato la polvere: He's no great shakes; he'll never set the world on fire.
LIT. He hasn't invented (gun) powder.

PONTE (IL) Bridge

A nemico che fugge, ponti d'oro
LIT. To fleeing foe, bridges of gold.

Ma dagli pure la liquidazione che vuole! *A nemico che fugge . . .* (Go ahead and give him all the severance pay he wants. Anything to get rid of him!)

Far ponti d'oro a qualcuno: To make things as easy and attractive as possible for someone.
LIT. To make bridges of gold to someone.

Sfido che ha accettato il posto! L'azienda *gli ha fatto ponti d'oro.* (I don't wonder he took the job. Nobody could have turned down that kind of offer.)

Tagliare i ponti: To break off relations; to burn one's bridges.
LIT. To cut one's bridges.

POPOLO (IL) People

Coram populo
LIT. (Latin for) In front of everybody.

E ha avuto il coraggio di dirmelo *coram populo!* (And he had the nerve to tell me right there in public!)

Popolo e comune: Everybody and his brother.
LIT. The people and the town.

Lei spera ancora di poterlo tener segreto e invece lo sa *popolo e comune.* (She's still hoping to keep it quiet, when the whole town's talking about it.)

PORTA (LA) Door

Essere alle porte coi sassi: To be very close to a deadline.
LIT. To be at the doors with the stones.

Quando pensi di metterti al lavoro? Guarda che *siamo alle porte coi sassi.* (When are you planning to get to work? There isn't much time left, you know.)

Mettere qualcuno alla porta: To show someone the door; to throw someone out.
LIT. To put someone at the door.

Sfondare una porta aperta: To speak eagerly in defense of a cause that needs no support.
LIT. To crash through an open door.

Vuoi persuadermi che è un ragazzo in gamba? Mio caro, *sfondi una porta aperta.* (You don't have to convince me. I've been a supporter of his for years.)

PORTO (IL) Port, harbor

Condurre in porto, condurre a buon porto: To accomplish successfully.
LIT. To bring into port; to bring into good port.

Porto di mare: Said of a place where people are continually coming and going.
LIT. Sea port.

Quando i ragazzi sono in vacanza, la nostra casa è un *porto di mare.* (When the children are on vacation, our house is like Grand Central Station.)

POSTO (IL) Place

Mettere a posto qualcosa: To put something back where it belongs.
LIT. To put something in place.

Mettere a posto qualcuno: To put someone in his place.
LIT. To put someone in place.

Una persona a posto: A solid, reliable person.
LIT. A person in place.

Non me lo sarei mai aspettato. *Una persona così a posto!* (I can't believe it. He seemed like such a nice man!)

POVERO Poor

Povero in canna: Poor as a churchmouse.
LIT. Poor in reed.

POZZO (IL) Well

Far vedere la luna nel pozzo (See **Luna**)

Pozzo di scienza: Pillar of learning.
LIT. Well of science.

PRENDERE To take

Prender cappello (See **Cappello**)

Prendere due piccioni con una fava: To kill two birds with one stone.
LIT. To take two pigeons with one bean.

Prendere in castagna qualcuno: To catch someone red-handed.
LIT. To take someone in chestnut.

Prendere per l'ingiù: To take a dislike to.
LIT. To take upside down.

È una ragazza simpatica. Peccato mia madre *l'abbia presa per l'ingiù.* (She's a nice girl. Too bad my mother has taken a dislike to her.)

Prendere qualcosa o qualcuno con le pinze, prendere qualcosa o qualcuno con le molle: To take something or someone with a great many reservations; with disgust.
LIT. To take something or someone with tongs.

In un'intervista svoltasi in queste condizioni, le risposte son *da prendersi con le molle.* (In an interview under these conditions, I would have serious reservations about the answers.) Guarda che è un essere spregevole, *da prendersi con le molle.* (Watch out, he's an awful person. I wouldn't touch him with a ten-foot pole!)

Prendere qualcuno per il suo verso: To humor someone; to play it his way.

LIT. To take someone by his way.

Non è veramente così difficile. Bisogna saperla *prendere per il suo verso*. (She's not really so bad. You just have to know how to handle her.)

Prendere una cantonata: To make a mistake and refuse to admit it.

LIT. To take a street corner.

È inutile, *ha preso una cantonata* e non c'è niente da fare. (I'm afraid he just made a big mistake and there's no talking him out of it.)

Prendere una cattiva piega: To take a bad turn; to develop bad habits.

LIT. To take a bad fold.

Prendere *una papera*

Prendere una papera, prendere un granchio: To blunder; to goof; to pull a boner.

LIT. To take a duck; to take a crab.

Prendersela calma: To take one's time; to take it easy.

LIT. To take it calm.

PRETE (IL) Priest

Fa quel che il prete dice, ma non far quel che il prete fa: Do as I say, not as I do.

LIT. Do what the priest says but don't do what the priest does.

Scherzo da prete (See **Scherzo**)

PREZZEMOLO (IL) Parsley

Essere come il prezzemolo: To get around a great deal; to be a busybody.

LIT. To be like parsley.

PUGNO (IL) Fist

Di proprio pugno: In one's own handwriting.
LIT. Of one's own fist.

Fare a pugni: To fight; also said of colors that clash.
LIT. To make at fists.

> Fammi il piacere di levarti quel golf. *Fa a pugni* con la camicetta. (Do me a favor and take off that sweater. I can't stand the way it clashes with that blouse.)

Rimanere con un pugno di mosche (See **Mosca**)

PULCINELLA Name of mask from Commedia dell'Arte

Segreto di Pulcinella: Open secret.
LIT. Pulcinella's secret.

PULCINO (IL) Chick

Essere un pulcino bagnato: To be a sissy; a fraidy cat.
LIT. To be a wet chick.

Essere un pulcino nella stoppa: To be a babe in the woods.
LIT. To be a chick in the tow.

PULPITO (IL) Pulpit

Senti da che pulpito viene la predica: Look who's talking!
LIT. Hear from what pulpit comes the sermon.

PUNTO (IL) Point, period, dot, stitch

Dare dei punti a qualcuno: To be superior to someone.
LIT. To give points to someone.

> Quanto all'arte della persuasione, bisogna riconoscere che può *dare dei punti* a chiunque. (As far as persuasiveness goes, you'll have to admit that he's second to nobody.)

Di punto in bianco: Suddenly; out of nowhere.
LIT. Of point in white.

Di tutto punto: Completely.
LIT. Of all point.

> È venuto fuori vestito *di tutto punto.* (He arrived impeccably dressed.)

Essere a buon punto: To be well along in an undertaking.
LIT. To be at good point.

Fare il punto: To take a ship's bearing; to take stock.
LIT. To make the point.

Fare punto: To stop; to call it a day.
LIT. To do period.

In punto: On (the) dot.

Mettere i puntini sugli i: To dot one's *i*'s and cross one's *t*'s.

Per un punto Martin perdé la cappa*: For want of a nail, the miller lost his mare; a miss is as good as a mile.
LIT. For a period Martin lost his cape.

Punto e basta: Period!
LIT. Period and enough.

Punto morto: Standstill, impasse.
LIT. Dead point.

---

* A reference to an error in punctuation that allegedly caused a monk to be defrocked.

Q

QUARTO Fourth

Partire in quarta: To take off on a tirade over something.
LIT. To leave in fourth (gear).

Non partire in quarta prima di aver capito di che cosa si
tratta. (Don't get all worked up over this before you find
out the facts.)

QUATTRO Four

Farsi in quattro: To go out of one's way for someone.
LIT. To make oneself in four.

Appena le ho detto che avevo bisogno di quel libro, *si è fatta in quattro* per procurarmelo. (As soon as I told her I needed that book, she went out of her way to get it for me.)

In quattro e quattr'otto: In no time.
LIT. In four and four eight.

Mangiare a quattro palmenti (See **Palmento**)

Non dir quattro finché non l'hai nel sacco: Don't count your chickens before they are hatched.
LIT. Don't say four till you have it in the bag.

Spaccare un capello in quattro (See **Capello**)

Farsi in quattro

R

RADICE (LA) Root

Metter radici: To settle down in a place, a job, etc. and not budge.
LIT. To put roots.

> Andiamo a casa, via. Che succede, *ci hai messo radici?*
> (Come on now, let's go home. What's the matter with you, do you want to sleep here?)

RAGIONE (LA) Reason

A ragion veduta: Everything considered.
LIT. At reason seen.

> Lo dico *a ragion veduta.* (It's my considered opinion.)

Darle di santa ragione a qualcuno: To give someone a good beating.

LIT. To give them with holy reason to someone.

Farsi una ragione di qualcosa: To learn to accept something; to become reconciled to it.
LIT. To make oneself a reason of something.

> Credo che in principio ne abbia sofferto molto, ma ormai *se ne è fatta una ragione.* (I believe she had a very bad time at the beginning, but recently she's come to terms with it.)

RAMO (IL) Branch

Avere un rametto: To be a little nutty.
LIT. To have a little branch.

> Mi sbaglio o quel tuo amico *ha un rametto?* (Could I be wrong, or is that friend of yours slightly off his rocker?)

RASOIO (IL) Razor

Camminare sul filo di un rasoio: To walk on the razor's edge; to skate on thin ice.

RAZZA (LA) Race

Che razza di ———!
LIT. What a race of ———.

> *Che razza di furfante!* (He's one hell of a rascal!) *Che razza di* faccia tosta! (He's got some nerve, I'm telling you!)

REALISTA Realist, royalist

Essere più realista del re: To be more royalist than the King.

REGOLA (LA) Rule

A regola d'arte: To perfection.
LIT. At art's rule.

> Brava! Questa cucitura è fatta proprio *a regola d'arte.*

(Wonderful! This seam looks like the work of a professional.)

Con tutte le regole, in piena regola: Complete, first class.
LIT. With all the rules; in full rule.

Mi sembra che questo signore sia un truffatore *in piena regola.* (I think this Mr. Smith is a swindler, if I ever saw one.)

Farsi una regola di: To make a point of.
LIT. To make oneself a rule of.

L'eccezione conferma la regola: The exception confirms the rule.

Per tua norma e regola: For your information.
LIT. For your norm and rule.

Per tua norma e regola, questi discorsi in casa mia non s'erano mai fatti. (If you really must know, this is not the kind of talk we usually have in our house.)

RICCO Rich

Essere ricco sfondato: To be rolling in money.
LIT. To be bottomless rich.

RIGA (LA) Line

Leggere fra le righe: To read between the lines.

RIMA (LA) Rhyme

Rispondere per le rime: To give as good as one gets.
LIT. To answer by the rhymes.

RISATA (LA) Laugh

Fare le grasse risate su o di qualcosa: To laugh ostentatiously about something deemed preposterous or ridiculous.
LIT. To do the fat laughs about something.

Che non lo sappia, per carità, ma noi *ci abbiamo fatto sopra le grasse risate!* (Don't ever tell him, for God's sake, but we really had a good laugh over it!)

RISCIACQUATA (LA) Rinse

Dare una risciacquata a qualcuno: To give someone a good scolding.
LIT. To give someone a rinse.

RITRATTO (IL) Portrait

Essere il ritratto di qualcuno: To be the image of someone.
LIT. To be the portrait of someone.

ROBA (LA) Things, stuff

Bella roba: Nice work! (sarcastic)
LIT. Beautiful stuff.

Sei stato in città senza darmi neppure un colpo di telefono. *Bella roba!* (You were in town and didn't even call me up. Shame on you!)

Che roba: How awful!
LIT. What stuff.

Hai letto l'ultima sul conto di X? *Che roba!* (Did you read about X's latest escapade? Pretty awful, isn't it?)

ROMANO Roman

Fare alla romana: To go fifty-fifty; to go Dutch.
LIT. To do it the Roman way.

ROSA (LA) Rose

All'acqua di rose: Superficial; perfunctory.
LIT. By rose water.

Un professore *all'acqua di rose.* (A professor in name only.) Una punizione *all'acqua di rose.* (A mild punishment.)

Fresco come una rosa: Fresh as a daisy; bold, fresh.
LIT. Fresh as a rose.

È venuto a chiedermi, *fresco come una rosa,* se potevo

imprestargli di nuovo un libro. (He came to ask me, cool as a cucumber, if I'd lend him another book.)

Letto di rose: A bed of roses.

Rose e fiori: A cinch.
LIT. Roses and flowers.

Non son tutte *rose e fiori*. (It's not all beer and skittles.) In un lavoro come il mio, checché tu ne pensi, non sono tutte *rose e fiori*. (Regardless of what you say, a job like mine isn't all peaches and cream.)

Se saran rose fioriranno: We'll just have to wait and see; time will tell.
LIT. If they are roses they will bloom.

ROSPO (IL) Toad

Fare ingoiare un rospo: To ram something down someone's throat.
LIT. To make someone swallow a toad.

Ingoiare un rospo: To have to tolerate something unpleasant; to swallow a bitter pill.
LIT. To swallow a toad.

Sputare il rospo
LIT. To spit the toad.

Andiamo, via. *Sputa il rospo!* (Come on, let's have it out!)

ROTOLO (IL) Roll

Andare a rotoli (See also **andare a rotta di Collo**): To go to rack and ruin; to be in bad shape.
LIT. To go to rolls.

Tutto *va a rotoli*, son proprio disperato. (Everything's going to the dogs, and I'm really at my wit's end.)

RUGGINE (LA) Rust

Avere una vecchia ruggine: To have an old grudge; to have it in for someone.
LIT. To have an old rust.

RUOTA (LA) Wheel

A ruota: Close(ly); neck-and-neck.
LIT. By wheel.

Avere le rotelle fuori posto: To have a screw loose.
LIT. To have one's little wheels out of place.

Essere l'ultima ruota del carro (See **Carro**)

Fare la ruota: To bask in self-love and pride.
LIT. To do the wheel (like a peacock).

Mettere i bastoni fra le ruote: To thwart someone's efforts;
to put a spoke in someone's wheel.
LIT. To put sticks between the wheels.

Mettere i bastoni fra le ruote

Unger le ruote: To buy someone off; to grease someone's
palm.
LIT. To oil the wheels.

S

SABBIA (LA) Sand
Scrivere sulla sabbia: To write on sand.

SACCO (IL) Bag, sack

Cogliere qualcuno con le mani nel sacco (See **Mano**)

Comprare la gatta nel sacco (See **Gatto**)

Darne un sacco e una sporta: To give someone a good beating.
LIT. To give a sack and a bag of them.

Dirne un sacco e una sporta: To give someone a piece of one's mind.
LIT. To say a sack and a bag of them.

Farina del proprio sacco: Fruit of one's own labors.

LIT. Flour of one's own bag.

Dì la verità, questa non è *tutta farina del tuo sacco*. (Tell the truth! This isn't entirely your own work, is it?)

Far le cose con la testa nel sacco (See **Testa**)

Mettere a sacco: To sack, to plunder.
LIT. To put to sack.

Mettere qualcuno nel sacco: To deceive someone; to pull the wool over his eyes.
LIT. To put someone in the sack.

Reggere il sacco: To aid and abet someone in an illegal undertaking.
LIT. To hold the sack.

Dà retta a me, non ti far vedere in giro con un tipo di quel genere. La gente crederà che tu *gli regga il sacco*. (Take my advice, don't let people see you going around with a man like that. They'll think you're one of the gang.)

Tornare con le pive nel sacco: To come back empty-handed, frustrated, crestfallen.
LIT. To come back with the bag-pipes in the bag.

Glielo avevo detto ch'era una ragazza seria e che *sarebbe tornato con le pive nel sacco*. (I told him she wasn't that kind of girl and that he wouldn't be able to make any time with her.)

Vuotare il sacco: To make a clean breast of something; to get something off one's chest.
LIT. To empty the sack.

Scusami, sai, ma avevo proprio bisogno di *vuotare il sacco*. (Forgive me, but I just had to get it off my chest.)

SALE (IL) Salt

Aver sale in zucca: To have good common sense; to have a brain in one's head; to be nobody's fool.

LIT. To have salt in the pumpkin (head).

Cum grano salis: (Latin for) With a grain of salt.

Non metterci né sale né pepe: To refrain from giving one's opinion.
LIT. Not to put either salt or pepper in it.

> Per conto mio, *non ci metto né sale né pepe.* È una decisione che devono prendere da soli. (I, for one, intend to keep my suggestions to myself. This is a decision they'll have to make on their own.)

Restar di sale (See also **restar di Stucco, di Sasso**): To be left open-mouthed.
LIT. To be left of salt.

> Quando ho saputo la notizia, *son rimasto di sale.* (When I heard the news, you could have knocked me over with a feather.)

SALTO (IL) Jump

Far quattro salti: To get together for some very informal dancing.
LIT. To make four jumps.

> Andiamo a casa mia. Ho un nuovo giradischi e, se vogliamo, possiamo *fare quattro salti.* (Let's go to my house. I have a new hi-fi set and if we feel like it, we can dance.)

Fare un salto: To pop in; to go by.
LIT. To make a jump.

> Vuoi che *ci faccia un salto io?* Non mi costa niente, è a un passo da casa mia. (Do you want me to drop over there? It's no trouble, it's just around the corner from my house.)

SANGUE (IL) Blood

Cavar sangue da una rapa: To get blood from a stone.
LIT. To draw blood from a turnip.

Cavar sangue *da una rapa*

Far bollire il sangue nelle vene: To make one's blood boil.
LIT. To make one's blood boil in one's veins.

Far gelare il sangue nelle vene: To make one's blood run-cold.
LIT. To make one's blood freeze in one's veins.

Farsi cattivo sangue: To worry a great deal and bitterly over something.
LIT. To make bad blood for oneself.

È meglio non *farsi cattivo sangue,* tanto certe situazioni non si possono cambiare. (We might as well not eat our hearts out, there's nothing to be done about it, anyway.)

Il riso fa buon sangue: A good disposition makes one healthy.
LIT. Laughter makes good blood.

Il sangue non è acqua: Blood is thicker than water.
LIT. Blood is not water.

Con tutta la sua timidezza, hai visto che coraggio ha mostrato in questa occasione? Si vede proprio che *il sangue non è acqua.* (Shy as he is, don't you think he showed great courage in this instance? It just goes to show you, it runs in the family.)

Non aver sangue nelle vene: Not to have an ounce of spunk.
LIT. Not to have blood in one's veins.

Sangue freddo: Coolness; self-control.
LIT. Cold blood.

In certe occasioni, la cosa più importante è serbare *il*

sangue freddo. (In certain situations, the most important thing is to keep a cool head.)

SANTO (IL) Saint
Andare in paradiso a dispetto dei santi (See **Paradiso**)

Avere un santo dalla propria: To be extremely lucky; to have a guardian angel.
LIT. To have a saint on one's side.

I santi di casa non fanno miracoli: No one is considered a prophet in his own country.
LIT. Home saints work no miracles.

Gliel'ho detto, non aver paura, e gli ho anche portato un monte di buone ragioni. Ma sai

Avere un santo *dalla propria*

com'è, *i santi di casa* . . . È per questo che vorrei gli parlassi tu. (I told him, I can assure you, and I even gave him a dozen good reasons. But you know how it is, when you're one of the family . . . That's why I think it should come from you.)

Non essere uno stinco di santo: To be no saint.
LIT. Not to be a shinbone of a saint.

Non è uno stinco di santo neppure lui. (He's no angel either, you know.)

Non sapere a che santo votarsi: To be at one's wit's end; not to know where to turn.
LIT. Not to know what saint to devote oneself to.

Passata la festa gabbato lo santo (See **Festa**)

Sancta sanctorum: Very special place, to which only a few people have access.
LIT. (Latin for) Holy of holies.

È vero che ti ha lasciato entrare nel *sancta sanctorum,* la sua biblioteca? (Did he really let you in to the inner sanctum, his library?)

SAPERE To know, to taste of

Non sapere né di me né di te: To be tasteless, meaningless.
LIT. Not to taste of either me or you.

Saperci fare: To know one's way around; to know how to handle someone; to have a way with people.
LIT. To know how to do there.

È inutile, con mio padre bisogna *saperci fare.* (It's no use. You've got to know how to handle my father.)

Saperla lunga (See **Lungo**)

SAPONE (IL) Soap

Rimetterci il ranno e il sapone: To experience a total loss; to lose one's shirt.
LIT. To lose both lye and soap in it.

Se fossi te, mi terrei alla larga da tutto l'affare. C'è da *rimetterci ranno e sapone.* (If I were you, I'd stay clear of the whole business. You could end up losing your shirt.)

SASSO (IL) Stone

Essere alle porte coi sassi (See **Porta**)

Far piangere i sassi: To arouse great pity; to make someone's heart bleed.
LIT. To make the stones cry.

Una storia, ti assicuro, *da far piangere i sassi.* (A story, I tell you, that would break your heart.)

Restar di sasso (See also **restar di Sale, di Stucco**): To be left open-mouthed.

LIT. To remain of stone.

> Che vuoi, a sentirmi dire certe cose da una persona calma e cortese come lei, *ci son rimasto di sasso*. (What do you expect? I was flabbergasted to hear someone as kind as she is saying things like that.)

Tirar il sasso e nasconder la mano: To attack someone and then be unwilling to take the consequences.

LIT. To throw the stone and hide the hand.

> L'hai detto sì o no? Non mi farai quello che *tira il sasso e nasconde la mano!* (Did you say it or didn't you? I hope you have the courage of your convictions!)

Tirar sassi in piccionaia: To throw a stone in one's own garden; to foul one's own nest.

LIT. To throw stones into the pigeon coop.

SCACCO (LO) Check

Dare scacco matto a qualcuno: To defeat someone once and for all.

LIT. To give someone checkmate.

Subire uno scacco: To undergo a bitter defeat.

LIT. To suffer a check.

Tenere qualcuno in scacco: To hold someone in check.

SCAMPARE To escape

Scamparla bella: To have a narrow escape; a close shave.

LIT. To escape it beautiful.

SCAPPARE To escape

A scappa e fuggi: On the run, briefly.

LIT. At escape and flee.

> Ti dico, non so niente di niente. L'ho visto un momento appena, *a scappa e fuggi*. (I know absolutely nothing about it. I just saw him for a second.)

SCAPPATA (LA) Escape, escapade, run

Fare una scappata: To dash over and back; to take a short trip.
LIT. To make a flight.

> Non preoccupartene, *ci faccio una scappata* io domattina. (Don't worry about it. I'll pop over there in the morning and see what's what.)

SCARPA (LA) Shoe

Fare la scarpetta: To lick the plate clean.
LIT. To do the little shoe.

Fare le scarpe a uno (See also **fare le Calze**): To inform on someone.
LIT. To do the shoes to someone.

> Io certi commenti non li farei ad anima viva. Non si sa mai, domani magari vien fuori che *fai le scarpe* a un collega. (I wouldn't repeat this to a living soul, if I were you. The next thing you know, they're saying you want to do him out of a job.)

Lustrar le scarpe a qualcuno (See also **leccare i Piedi**): To lick someone's boots.
LIT. To polish someone's shoes.

Mettere le scarpe al sole: To die.
LIT. To put one's shoes in the sun.

Morire con le scarpe ai piedi: To die a violent or sudden death.
LIT. To die with one's shoes on.

> L'avevo sempre saputo che quello *moriva con le scarpe ai piedi.* (I always knew he'd come to a violent end.)

SCATOLA (LA) Box

Rompere le scatole a qualcuno: To bother someone; to be a pain in the neck.
LIT. To break the boxes to someone (rather crude).

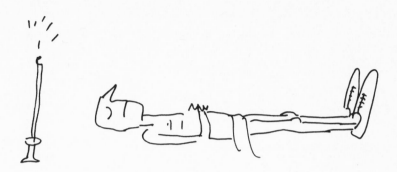

Morire con le scarpe *ai piedi*

Ma lo sai che *mi hai proprio rotto le scatole?* Fammi il favore, levati dai piedi! (You've really driven me crazy, you know! Do me a favor, get lost!)

Rompiscatole: Pain in the neck.
LIT. Breaker of boxes.

Ma che razza di *rompiscatole* è quel tuo amico! (What a pain in the neck that friend of yours is!)

SCENA (LA) Stage, scene

Calcare le scene: To tread the boards; to act in a theater.
LIT. To tread the stage.

Colpo di scena (See **Colpo**)

SCHERZO (LO) Trick, joke

Brutto scherzo: Dirty trick.
LIT. Ugly trick.

Scherzo da prete: Dirty trick.
LIT. Priest's trick.

Stare allo scherzo: To be game.
LIT. To stay at the game.

Scherzo *da prete*

SCILLA Scylla

Fra Scilla e Cariddi: Between Scylla and Charybdis; between the devil and the deep blue sea.

SCOPA (LA) Broom

Scopa nuova spazza bene: A new broom sweeps clean.
LIT. New broom sweeps well.

SCUFFIA (LA) Bonnet

Prendere una scuffia: To get drunk.
LIT. To take a bonnet.

SECCO Dry

Far secco qualcuno: To leave someone speechless with a forceful comment.
LIT. To make someone dry.

Lascia fare a me. Due paroline come le intendo io e *lo faccio secco.* (Leave it to me. I'll shut him up with a few well-chosen words.)

Murare a secco: Facetious reference to eating a meal without wine.
LIT. To build without mortar.

Restarci secco: To die, to give up the ghost.
LIT. To remain there dry.

SEDUTA (LA) Meeting, session

Seduta stante: Immediately; on the spot.
LIT. Meeting staying.

Gli ho risposto *seduta stante* che sarei stato felicissimo di accettare l'offerta. (I told him, without giving it a moment's thought, that I'd be happy to accept the offer.)

SEGGIOLA (LA) Chair

Sedere su due seggiole (See also **tener il piede in due Staffe**):

To sit on both sides of the fence.
LIT. To sit on two chairs.

SEGNO (IL) Mark

Aver passato il segno: To have gone too far.
LIT. To have passed the mark.

Cogliere nel segno: To hit the mark, the nail on the head, the bull's-eye.
LIT. To catch (hit) in the sign.

Sedere su due seggiole

SENNO (IL) Judgment, wisdom

Da senno: Seriously; in earnest.
LIT. By judgment.

Del senno di poi son piene le fosse: Everyone is wise after the event; hindsight is easier than foresight.
LIT. The ditches are full of the after-event wisdom.

Bravo lui! *Del senno di poi* . . . (How smart of him! Another Monday morning quarterback . . .)

Uscire di senno (See **Uscire**)

SENSO (IL) Sense, feeling, direction, meaning

Fare senso: To arouse disgust; to upset.
LIT. To make sense.

Come fai a toccare i vermi? Non ti *fanno senso?* (How can you bear to handle worms? Don't they make you sick?)

SERPE (LA) Serpent, snake

Allevare la serpe in seno, scaldare la serpe in seno: To nurse a viper in one's bosom.
LIT. To raise a snake in one's bosom; to warm a snake in one's bosom.

/ 189

Scaldare la serpe *in seno*

SETE (LA) Thirst

Levarsi la sete col prosciutto: To resort to a remedy worse than the ill. LIT. To quench one's thirst with ham.

SFIDARE To challenge, to defy

Sfido: No wonder! I should say so! LIT. I challenge.

Sfido che non è amato! Ha un carattere così cattivo. (No wonder he's not popular! He has such a bad disposition.) "Non trovi che ho avuto ragione?" "*Sfido!* Dopo tutto quel che ti aveva detto." ("Don't you think I was right?" "I should say so! After the things he said to you!")

SGAMBETTO (LO) Jump

Dare lo sgambetto a qualcuno: To undercut someone quietly in order to take his place. LIT. To give the jump to someone, to trip someone.

Intendiamoci, solo se il posto c'è. Non voglio mica *dar lo sgambetto a qualcuno*. (Only if the position is available, of course. I don't want to have anyone kicked out for my sake.)

SGOCCIOLO (LO) Dripping

Essere agli sgoccioli: To be at the very end of something. LIT. To be at the drippings.

Il denaro mandatogli dai suoi *è ormai agli sgoccioli*. (The money he got from his family is just about gone.)

SÌ Yes

Sì e no: At the most.

LIT. Yes and no.

Quest'inverno sono andato a teatro *sì e no* quattro volte. (This winter I've been to the theater four times at the most.)

SINE (Latin for) Without

Sine qua non: Indispensable condition.
LIT. Without which not.

Pare che ne abbia fatto addirittura *un sine qua non* di tutto l'accordo. (Apparently, the whole agreement hinges on it.)

SODO Hard

Venire al sodo: To come to the point; to get down to brass tacks.
LIT. To come to the hard.

SOFFRIRE To suffer

Non poter soffrire qualcuno o qualcosa: Not to be able to stand someone or something.
LIT. Not to be able to suffer someone or something.

Per carità, non mi dare caffè. *Non lo posso soffrire.* (For goodness' sake, don't give me any coffee. I can't stand it!)

SOGNO (IL) Dream

Nemmeno per sogno! (See also **nemmeno per Ombra**): I wouldn't dream of it! Not in the least!
LIT. Not even for dream.

Un viaggio con lui? *Nemmeno per sogno!* (Take a trip with him? Not on your life!)

SOLE (IL) Sun

Avere qualcosa al sole: To own a little land.
LIT. To have something out in the sun.

Prima di morire, mi piacerebbe di *aver qualcosa al sole*.
(Before I die, I'd love to call a piece of land my own.)

Cercare il sole a mezzanotte: To want the impossible.
LIT. To look for the sun at midnight.

Farsi bello del sol d'agosto (See **Bello**)

Vedere il sole a scacchi: To be in jail.
LIT. To see the sun in squares.

SOLO Alone

Meglio solo che male accompagnato: Better alone than in bad company.

SONNO (IL) Sleep

Avere il sonno duro: To be a sound sleeper; to sleep like the dead.
LIT. To have the sleep hard.

SORCIO (IL) Mouse

Far la fine del sorcio: To get trapped.
LIT. To do the end of a mouse.

Far vedere i sorci verdi: To do extraordinary and unexpected things.
LIT. To show the green mice.

> Cosa? Vuoi ballare? Stasera ci *fai proprio vedere i sorci verdi!* (What? You want to dance? Well, tonight we'll have seen everything!)

Quando il gatto è fuori i sorci ballano (See **Gatto**)

SORDO Deaf

Cantarla ai sordi: To try to talk sense to someone who won't listen.
LIT. To sing it to deaf people.

Non c'è peggior sordo di chi non vuol sentire: There's no one as deaf as he who won't listen.

Non dirlo a un sordo: To suggest something which is eagerly accepted.

LIT. Not to say it to a deaf man.

Hai sentito le sue teorie sull'imprestare i libri? *Non l'ha detto a un sordo.* Aspetta che mi chieda di nuovo di portarmi via un libro antico! (Did you hear him expounding on the wisdom of never lending books? It didn't fall on deaf ears. I'll bear it in mind the next time he asks me for a first edition!)

Sordo come una campana, sordo come un banco: As deaf as a post, as a dormouse, as a knob.
LIT. Deaf as a bell, as a bench.

Sordo spaccato: Stone-deaf.
LIT. Deaf split.

SOSPIRARE To sigh, to long for

Farsi sospirare: To play hard to get; to be long in coming.
LIT. To make oneself be longed for.

SOTTILE Slim, subtle

Non guardar per il sottile: Not to be too choosy.
LIT. Not to look for the subtle.

Se non è bella, non importa. *Non guardo tanto per il sottile.* Quel che mi preme è che sia brava. (If she's not good-looking, I couldn't care less. I'm not so hard to please, as long as she's a hard worker.)

SPADA (LA) Sword

Difendere a spada tratta: To defend a person or a cause staunchly and passionately.

Difendere a spada *tratta*

LIT. To defend with drawn sword.

Mettere a fil di spada: To put to the sword.
LIT. To put at the sword's edge.

Spada di Damocle*: Sword of Damocles; constant threat of imminent danger.

> Preferisco farne a meno piuttosto che vivere sotto *la spada di Damocle* delle rate mensili. (I'd rather do without than have those monthly payments hanging over my head.)

SPAGO (LO) String

> **Dar spago** (See also **dar Corda**): To encourage someone to talk; to lead him on.

Dar spago

LIT. To give string.

> Se *gli dai spago*, ti tien lì tutta la notte. (If you encourage him, he'll keep you there all night.)

SPALLA (LA) Shoulder

---

* A reference to the lesson given to Damocles by the elder Dionysius of Syracuse.

Alle spalle di qualcuno: At someone's expense.
LIT. At the shoulders of someone.

> Ci siamo fatti una buona risata *alle sue spalle.* (We had a good laugh on him.)

Aver le spalle larghe: To be able to take a lot of responsibility or criticism.
LIT. To have broad shoulders.

Aver la testa sulle spalle: To have a (good) head on one's shoulders.

Aver qualcuno sulle spalle (See also **aver qualcuno a Carico**): To have to support someone.
LIT. To have someone on one's shoulders.

Buttarsi qualcosa dietro le spalle: To neglect something; to postpone taking care of it.
LIT. To throw something behind one's shoulders.

> Sai com'è fatto . . . se una pratica non è urgente, *se la butta dietro le spalle.* (You know how he is . . . if a case isn't urgent, he just lets it slide.)

Dietro le spalle: Behind one's back.
LIT. Behind one's shoulders.

Fare spallucce: To shrug off impatiently someone's suggestions or comments.
LIT. To make little shoulders.

Mettere qualcuno con le spalle al muro: To back someone into a corner.
LIT. To put someone with his shoulders to the wall.

Stringersi nelle spalle: To shrug one's shoulders in doubt or indifference.
LIT. To squeeze oneself in one's shoulders.

Vivere alle spalle di qualcuno: To live off someone.
LIT. To live at someone's shoulders.

SPASSO (LO) Walk, pastime, fun
Essere a spasso: To be unemployed.

LIT. To be out for a walk.

Mandare a spasso qualcuno: To get rid of someone; to dismiss him.
LIT. To send someone for a walk.

Portare a spasso qualcuno: To take someone for a ride.
LIT. To take someone for a walk.

Prendersi spasso di qualcuno: To make fun of someone.
LIT. To take pastime of someone.

SPECCHIO (LO) Mirror

Arrampicarsi sugli specchi: To go to any lengths to defend an untenable position.
LIT. To climb up on the mirrors.

> Finiscila, via! Ti stai proprio *arrampicando sugli specchi*. (Come on, stop it! You know you don't have a leg to stand on.)

SPENDERE To spend

Spendere e spandere: To spend extravagantly.
LIT. To spend and spread.

> È difficile fare economia quando si viaggia con uno che *spende e spande*. (It's hard to save money when you travel with someone who throws his money around.)

SPESA (LA) Expense, shopping

È più la spesa che l'impresa: It's more trouble than it's worth.
LIT. The expense is more than the undertaking.

Fare le spese di una conversazione, di una serata: To be the main topic of conversation, especially in absentia.
LIT. To do the expense of a conversation, of an evening.

> Sai che ieri sera le tue imprese amorose *hanno fatto le spese* della conversazione? (Did you know that your love life was the main topic of last night's conversation?)

SPETTACOLO (LO) Performance

Dare spettacolo: To make a spectacle of oneself.
LIT. To give performance.

> Aspettiamo a litigarci quando siamo a casa. *Non diamo spettacolo.* (Let's wait to argue about it when we get home. Let's not put on a show for everyone.)

SPINA (LA) Thorn

Essere sulle spine (See also **essere sui Carboni ardenti**): To be on pins and needles; on tenterhooks.
LIT. To be on the thorns.

Una spina nel fianco (See also **pruno in un Occhio**): A thorn in one's side, in the flesh.

Essere sulle spine

SPOLA (LA) Shuttle

Fare la spola: To shuttle back and forth.
LIT. To do the shuttle.

> Ho passato dei mesi *facendo la spola* fra ufficio e ospedale. (I spent all my time, for months, going back and forth from my office to the hospital.)

SPRONE (LO) Spur

A spron battuto: Full speed ahead.
LIT. At beaten spur.

> Come! Mi telefoni, io mi precipito *a spron battuto* . . . solo per questo? (What! You make me rush down here for this?)

SPUGNA (LA) Sponge

Bere come una spugna (See also **bere come un Turco**): To drink like a fish.
LIT. To drink like a sponge.

Buttare la spugna: To throw in the sponge, the towel.

Passare la spugna sopra: To let bygones be bygones.
LIT. To pass a sponge over.

> *Passiamoci la spugna sopra* e non pensiamoci più. (Let's let bygones be bygones and forget all about it.)

SPUTARE To spit

Nato e sputato: The spitting image; a born (writer, painter, etc.).
LIT. Born and spit.

> Ma sentilo come parla bene! Un avvocato *nato e sputato!* (Listen to him talk! What a lawyer he'd make!)

Sputar sentenze: To make pompous statements.
LIT. To spit pronouncements.

> Non basta che sia uno stupido, deve anche *sputar sentenze* a destra e a sinistra. (Not only is he an idiot, he has to deliver big pronouncements right and left.)

SQUAGLIARE To melt

Squagliarsi: To sneak out.
LIT. To melt away.

STAFFA (LA) Stirrup

Bicchiere della staffa: Stirrup cup; one for the road.
LIT. Glass of the stirrup.

Perdere le staffe: To lose one's temper.
LIT. To lose the stirrups.

Tenere i piedi in due staffe (See also **sedere su due Seggiole**): To sit on both sides of the fence.
LIT. To keep one's feet in two stirrups.

Perdere le staffe

STAMPA (LA) Press

Avere buona stampa, avere cattiva stampa: To have a good reputation, to have a bad reputation.
LIT. To have good press, to have bad press.

STAMPO (LO) Mold

D'antico stampo: In the old-fashioned grand manner.
LIT. Of old mold.

Un signore *d'antico stampo.* (A gentleman of the old school.)

Di quegli uomini se n'è perduto lo stampo: They broke the mold after they made him.
LIT. Of those men they have lost the mold.

Son tutti d'uno stampo: They're all the same; they're all cut from the same cloth.
LIT. They are all of one mold.

STARE To be, to stay

Stare sulle sue: To be unresponsive, overly reserved, aloof.
LIT. To stay on one's own.

Non ti è parso che *stesse un po' sulle sue?* (Didn't you think he was a little cool?)

STATO (LO) State, condition

Essere in stato interessante: To be pregnant.
LIT. To be in interesting condition.

STECCO (LO) Stick

Tenere a stecchetto: To keep someone on short rations of food or money.
LIT. To keep someone at small stick.

Se i genitori *lo tenessero un po' più a stecchetto,* farebbe meno sciocchezze. (If his parents gave him a little less money, he wouldn't get into so much trouble.)

STELLA (LA) Star

Portare qualcuno alle stelle: To rave about someone.
LIT. To take someone to the stars.

Se sentissi il suo principale. *Lo porta addirittura alle stelle.* (You should hear his boss. He thinks the world of him.)

Vedere le stelle: To see stars.

STOFFA (LA) Fabric

Aver la stoffa di: To have the makings of.
LIT. To have the fabric of.

STORIA (LA) Story, history

Fare storie: To carry on about something; to make a fuss.
LIT. To make stories.

Portare qualcuno alle stelle

Ha fatto tante di quelle storie, che ho dovuto prometterle di accompagnarla io. (She carried on so that I had to promise to take her there myself.)

STRETTE (LE) Narrows

Mettere alle strette: To corner someone; to pin him down.
LIT. To put someone at the narrows.

STRUZZO (LO) Ostrich

Aver lo stomaco di struzzo: To have an infinite capacity for food.
LIT. To have the stomach of an ostrich.

Fare lo struzzo: To refuse to face reality; to bury one's head in the sand.

LIT. To do the ostrich.

STUCCO (LO) Stucco

Restar di stucco (See also **restar di Sale, di Sasso**): To be left open-mouthed.

LIT. To remain of stucco.

T

TABULA (Latin for) Tablet

Fare tabula rasa: To make a clean sweep in order to start afresh.
LIT. To make a shaved (clean) tablet.

TACCO (IL) Heel

Alzare il tacco, battere il tacco: To flee; to show a clean pair of heels.
LIT. To raise the heel, to beat the heel.

Girare i tacchi: To turn on one's heel and leave.
LIT. To turn one's heels.

TAGLIARE To cut

Essere tagliato per: To be cut out for; to have a gift for.

È inutile, negli affari, se uno *non c'è tagliato* . . . (It's no use. If you don't have a head for business, you might as well give up.)

TALLONE (IL) Heel

Tallone d'Achille: Achilles' heel, vulnerable spot.

TAMBURO (IL) Drum

A tambur battente: Immediately; on the double.
LIT. While the drum is pounding.

È fatto così: un angelo, ma i suoi ordini bisogna eseguirli *a tambur battente.* (That's the way he is—a heart of gold, but he likes everything done on the double.)

TAPPA (LA) Lap of a race, leg of a journey

Bruciar le tappe: To cut corners; to move quickly disregarding customary procedure.
LIT. To burn the laps.

Non possiamo star qui a discutere. Si tratta di cosa urgente e bisogna *bruciar le tappe.* (We can't sit here arguing about details. We have to act now and ask questions later.)

TAPPETO (IL) Carpet

Mettere sul tappeto: To bring up for discussion.
LIT. To put on the carpet.

TAPPEZZERIA (LA) Tapestry

Far tappezzeria: To be a wallflower.
LIT. To do (act) as tapestry.

TASCA (LA) Pocket

Aver le lacrime in tasca (See **Lacrima**)

Aver piene le tasche di: To be fed up with.
LIT. To have one's pockets full of.

Conoscere qualcuno o qualcosa come le proprie tasche: To

know someone or something inside out, like the back of one's hand.
LIT. To know someone or something like one's own pockets.

Rompere le tasche a qualcuno (See also **rompere le Scatole**): To irritate someone; to annoy the hell out of someone.
LIT. To break someone's pockets.

Star con le mani in tasca (See **Mano**)

TASTO (**IL**) Key (piano, typewriter)

Battere sempre sullo stesso tasto: To keep harping on the same subject.
LIT. To beat always on the same key.

Toccare un tasto doloroso: To touch a sore spot; to bring up a sore subject.
LIT. To touch a painful key.

TEMPO (**IL**) Time, weather, rhythm

A tempo e luogo: At the (proper) time and place.

A tempo perso: In one's spare time; at odd moments.
LIT. At lost time.

Aver fatto il proprio tempo: To have had one's day.
LIT. To have made one's time.

> Eran metodi tutt'altro che cattivi, ma *hanno fatto il loro tempo*. Oggi ci vuole qualcosa di nuovo. (They were good devices at the time, but we have to think of a more imaginative approach.)

Buontempone: Easy-going, fun-loving person.
LIT. Big good-timer.

Col tempo e con la paglia (See **Paglia**)

Con l'andare del tempo: In the long run; as time wears on.
LIT. With the going of time.

Dare tempo al tempo: To let things take their course.

LIT. To give time to time.

> Non puoi pretendere che cambi da un giorno all'altro. Bisogna *dar tempo al tempo*. (You can't expect him to change overnight. Be patient, and time will take care of it.)

Darsi buon tempo, darsi bel tempo: To have a jolly good time.
LIT. To give oneself good time.

Far la pioggia e il bel tempo (See **Pioggia**)

Guadagnar tempo: To play for time; to save time.
LIT. To earn time.

Il tempo stringe: Time is short.
LIT. Time tightens.

Ingannare il tempo: To kill time.
LIT. To cheat time.

Lasciare il tempo che si trova: To cause no change; to fail to affect the situation.
LIT. To leave the weather one finds.

> So bene che le mie parole *lasciano il tempo che trovano*. (I know very well that my words won't change a thing.)

O tempora o mores: What times we live in! We've come to a pretty pass!
LIT. (Latin for) What times, what customs.

Segnare il tempo: To mark time.

Senza metter tempo in mezzo: Without a moment's delay.
LIT. Without putting time in between.

Stringere i tempi: To make it snappy; to get something done in a hurry.
LIT. To tighten the rhythm.

> Qui, se non *stringiamo un po' i tempi,* non si arriva mica a terminare per la fine del mese. (Hey, if we don't get moving on this, we'll never be done by the end of the month.)

Temporibus illis: A long time ago.
LIT. (Latin for) In those times.

Sì, *temporibus* . . . ho lavorato per lui. Chi se ne ricorda più! (Yes, I did work for him once, but it's been more years than I care to remember!)

TENDA (LA) Curtain, drape, tent

Levare le tende: To break camp; to leave.
LIT. To take away one's tents.

Piantar le tende: To pitch one's tents.
LIT. To plant one's tents.

TENERO Tender

Esserci del tenero: Said of a romantic bond detected between two people.
LIT. To be some tender in it.

Non mi meraviglierei che fra i due *ci fosse del tenero.* (I wouldn't be surprised if there were a little romance going on between those two.)

TERRA (LA) Earth, ground, soil

Cercarle di sottoterra: To look for trouble.
LIT. To look for them underground.

Che cosa ti fa pensare che non ricorderà l'appuntamento? Le vai proprio a *cercare di sottoterra!* (What makes you think he'll forget to come? You really go out of your way to torment yourself, don't you?)

Correre ventre a terra: To run like mad; to ride like mad.
LIT. To run belly to the ground.

Ecco la lettera. Mi raccomando, *ventre a terra.* (Here's the letter, and, please, get it there as fast as you can.)

Far la terra per i ceci: To push up daisies.
LIT. To make soil for the beans.

Sentirsi mancare la terra sotto i piedi: To feel the ground give way under one's feet.

Terra terra: Limited, commonplace.
LIT. Earth earth.

Non è antipatico, ma molto *terra terra.* (He's not a bad guy, but nothing to write home about.)

Voler essere a cento piedi sotto terra: To be terribly ashamed or embarrassed.
LIT. To wish oneself one hundred feet underground.

Quando mi ha fatto quella domanda, *avrei voluto essere a cento piedi sotto terra!* (When he asked me that question, I wished I could sink right through the floor!)

TERRENO (IL) Ground, terrain

Tastare il terreno: To put out some feelers; to reconnoiter.
LIT. To feel (touch) the ground.

TESTA (LA) Head

Aver la testa per aria (See **Aria**)

Aver la testa tra le nuvole: To have one's head in the clouds.

Colpo di testa: Rash act.
LIT. Head blow.

Costare un occhio della testa (See **Occhio**)

Essere una testa per aria (See **Aria**)

Essere una testa quadra: To have a good head on one's shoulders.
LIT. To be a square head.

Far di testa propria: To follow one's own views against other people's advice to the contrary.
LIT. To do of one's own head.

Hai voluto fare di testa tua? Subiscine le conseguenze! (You made your bed, now lie in it!)

Fare a testa e croce: To play heads or tails; to toss a coin.
LIT. To do at head and cross.

Far le cose con la testa nel sacco: To act blindly; to do things as they come, unaware of the consequences.
LIT. To do things with one's head in the bag.

Credevo avessi preso tutte le informazioni necessarie. Possibile tu *faccia sempre le cose con la testa nel sacco?* (I assumed you'd gotten all the necessary data. Why don't you ever think anything through?)

Farsi una testa: To get all wrought up about something.
LIT. To make oneself a head.

Non te ne fare una testa, ché troveremo una soluzione. (Don't you go and worry about it. I'm sure we'll find a way out.)

Fasciarsi la testa

Fasciarsi la testa: To cry out before being hurt.
LIT. To bandage one's head.

Via, *non ti fasciare la testa!* Vedrai che sarai ricevuto benissimo e che non ci saranno problemi. (Come on, don't plan for the worst! I'm sure they'll be very cooperative and the problem will never arise.)

Levarsi qualcosa dalla testa (See **Levare**)

Metter la testa a partito (See **Partito**)

Montare la testa a qualcuno: To get someone excited; to put ideas into someone's head.
LIT. To whip up someone's head.

Poveretto, è una brava persona. Peccato che *gli abbiano*

montato la testa. (He's really a nice guy. It's a pity they've put ideas into his head.)

Montarsi la testa: To get a swelled head; to get excited.
LIT. To whip up one's head.

Rompersi la testa (See also **lambiccarsi il Cervello**): To rack one's brains.
LIT. To break one's head.

Tener testa a qualcuno: To hold one's own against someone.
LIT. To keep head to someone.

Testa di ponte: Beach-head.
LIT. Bridge head.

TESTO (IL) Text

Fare testo: To be an authority.
LIT. To make text.

L'ho saputo da X e in fatto di antropologia le sue parole *fanno testo.* (I heard it from X, and you must know that in the field of anthropology his word is law.)

TETTO (IL) Roof

Far la finestra sul tetto a qualcuno (See **Finestra**)

Il tetto è basso: Little pitchers have big ears.
LIT. The roof is low.

Va bene, ne parleremo più tardi. Ricordatevi che *il tetto è basso.* (Fine, we'll talk about it later. Remember the c-h-i-l-d is around.)

TIFO (IL) Typhus

Fare il tifo per qualcuno: To root for someone.
LIT. To make the typhus for someone.

TIPO (IL) Type, kind

Che tipo! Bel tipo: What a character!
LIT. What a type, beautiful type.

Lo sai che sei un *bel tipo?* (There are times when you really floor me!)

TOPO (IL) Mouse

Topo d'albergo: Thief specializing in hotel robberies.
LIT. Hotel mouse.

Topo di biblioteca: Bookworm.
LIT. Library mouse.

TORO (IL) Bull

Prendere il toro per le corna: To take the bull by the horns.

Tagliare la testa al toro: To settle something once and for all.

Tagliare la testa al toro

LIT. To cut the bull's head.

Hai fatto bene a dirmelo. Ero indeciso sul da farsi e questo *taglia la testa al toro*. (It's a good thing you told me. I didn't quite know what to do, but this settles it.)

TORTO (IL) Wrong, fault, error

Aver torto marcio: To be dead wrong.
LIT. To have rotten wrong.

TRAMONTANA (LA) North wind

Perdere la tramontana: To lose one's head.
LIT. To lose the North wind.

TRAVEGGOLE (LE) Disease of the eye

Aver le traveggole: To see double; to imagine things.
LIT. To have the "traveggole."

TRISTO Wicked

Il tristo nominato e visto: Speak of the devil!
LIT. The wicked one, mentioned and seen.

TROPPO Too much

Essere di troppo: To be in the way.
LIT. To be of too much.

Verrei volentieri, ma ho paura d'*essere di troppo*. (I'd like to come, but I wouldn't want to impose.)

TURCO (IL) Turk

Bere come un turco (See also **bere come una Spugna**): To drink like a fish.
LIT. To drink like a Turk.

Bestemmiare come un turco: To swear like a trooper.
LIT. To swear like a Turk.

Testa di turco: Butt of ridicule or teasing.
LIT. Turk's head.

Se credete di poter far di me la vostra *testa di turco,* vi sbagliate. (If you think you're going to make me the fall guy, you're mistaken.)

TUTTO All, everything

Giocare il tutto per tutto: To risk everything for the sake of an important goal.
LIT. To play everything for everything.

> *Ho giocato il tutto per tutto* e gli ho detto la verità. (I took a big chance and decided to tell him the truth.)

In tutto e per tutto: Exactly; completely.
LIT. In all and for all.

> Sono d'accordo con te *in tutto e per tutto.* (I agree with you one hundred percent.)

Tutt'al più: At the most.
LIT. All at the most.

> Telegrafargli, mai! *Tutt'al più, scrivigli.* (Send him a wire? Never. If you really must, write him a letter.)

U

UBRIACO Drunk

Ubriaco fradicio: Dead drunk.
LIT. Soaking drunk.

UCCELLO (**L'**) Bird

A volo d'uccello (See **Volo**)

Meglio uccel di bosco che uccel di gabbia: A hard life in freedom is better than a comfortable one in servitude.
LIT. Better a forest bird than a cage bird.

Uccel di bosco: Someone in hiding from the law; someone difficult to trace.
LIT. Forest bird.

Uccel di gabbia: Jailbird.
LIT. Cage bird.

UOVO (L') Egg

Camminare sulle uova (See **Camminare**)

Meglio un uovo oggi che una gallina domani: A bird in the hand is worth two in the bush.
LIT. Better an egg today than a hen tomorrow.

Pieno come un uovo: Full to the brim, chock full.
LIT. Full as an egg.

Rompere le uova nel paniere a qualcuno: To spoil someone's plans.
LIT. To break the eggs in someone's basket.

Ero appena riuscito a persuaderla di venire, quando è entrato lui a *rompermi le uova nel paniere.* (I had just convinced her to come along, when he walked in and the whole plan went down the drain.)

Rompere le uova *nel paniere*

Uovo di Colombo: A simple obvious idea that hasn't, however, occurred to the people concerned.
LIT. Columbus' egg.

Hai perfettamente ragione. *L'uovo di Colombo!* (You are so right. Why on earth didn't I think of it myself?)

URBS (Latin for) City

Urbi et orbi (See also **Popolo e comune**): Everybody and his brother
LIT. To the town and the world.

USCIO (L') Door, doorway

Avere male malanno e uscio addosso (See **Male**)

Esser a uscio e bottega: To live very close to someone; next door.
LIT. To be at door and shop.

Essere tra l'uscio e il muro: To be in a fix; to be forced to take action.
LIT. To be between the door and the wall.

Il peggior passo è quello dell'uscio: The first hundred years are the hardest.
LIT. The worst step is that of the door.

USCIRE To go out, to come out

Uscire dal seminato: To go off the subject.
LIT. To go out of the seeded field.

Essere tra l'uscio e il muro

Uscire dai gangheri: To fly off the handle.
LIT. To go off the hinges.

Uscir di mente: To slip one's mind.
LIT. To go out of mind.

Scusami tanto, *mi è proprio uscito di mente.* (I'm so sorry, it completely slipped my mind.)

Uscire di senno: To go out of one's mind.
LIT. To go out of one's judgment.

Uscire da un fianco: To be entirely unexpected news.
LIT. To go out from one's side.

Sposati? Questo proprio *mi esce da un fianco!* (They're married? That's the last thing I would have expected!)

V

VASO (IL) Vase, jar

La goccia che fa traboccare il vaso (See **Goccia**)

Portare vasi a Samo (See also **portare Acqua al mare**): To carry coals to Newcastle.
LIT. To bring vases to Samos.

VEDERE To see

Chi s'è visto s'è visto
LIT. Who has been seen, has been seen.

M'ha detto che il lavoro non l'interessava più e *chi s'è visto s'è visto!* (He just told me he was no longer interested in the job and that's the last I saw of him!)

Far vedere i sorci verdi (See **Sorcio**)

VELA (LA) Sail

Andare a gonfie vele: To go swimmingly.
LIT. To go with blown-up sails.

VELO (IL) Veil
Far velo: To obscure the truth.
LIT. To make veil.

> Non puoi dare un giudizio. Il tuo affetto per lui *ti fa velo.*
> (You're not in a position to judge. Your feelings for him
> make you biased.)

Stendere un velo sopra qualcosa: To avoid speaking about
something out of discretion or pity.
LIT. To draw a veil over something.

VENDERE To sell

Da vendere: More than one knows what to do with.
LIT. For sale.

> Ha ragione *da vendere!* (He's one hundred percent right!)
> Ha salute *da vendere.* (He's bursting with health.)

VENDETTA (LA) Revenge

Gridare vendetta: Said of an unusually wicked deed or an
unusually ugly object.
LIT. To scream revenge.

> Fra mobili antichi come i loro quel quadro astratto *grida
> vendetta!* (In a traditional living room, like theirs, that
> abstract horror is ludicrous.)

VENIRE To come

Il primo venuto: Complete stranger.
LIT. The first to come by.

> Come può sfogarsi così, col *primo venuto?* (How can she
> possibly go and pour her heart out to just anybody?)

VENTO (IL) Wind

Chi semina vento raccoglie tempesta: They that sow the wind shall reap the whirlwind; he who makes trouble will eventually have to suffer the consequences.
LIT. He who sows wind reaps storm.

Gridare ai quattro venti: To tell the world.
LIT. To scream to the four winds.

Pieno di vento: Full of hot air, windbag.
LIT. Full of wind.

Predicare al vento: To preach to the wind.

VERDE Green

Essere al verde: To be broke.
LIT. To be at the green.

VERO True

Non mi par vero di: I am delighted to; I can hardly wait to; I can hardly believe.
LIT. It doesn't seem true to me that.

Non mi par vero di rivederlo. (I can't wait to see him again.)

VESPAIO (IL) Beehive

Stuzzicare un vespaio: To stir up a hornet's nest.
LIT. To molest a beehive.

VIA (LA) Street, road, way

VIA Away

Dare il via: To give the starting signal; to give the green light.
LIT. To give the away.

Dar via libera: To give the green light.
LIT. To give free way.

E via dicendo: And so on.
LIT. And saying away.

Mettersi la via tra le gambe: To start on one's way.
LIT. To put the road between one's legs.

Non è la via dell'orto: Said of a long difficult road, or of an undertaking requiring time and skill.
LIT. It's not the path of the orchard.

> Abbi pazienza. Non è mica *la via dell'orto!* (Be patient, for God's sake. It's not as easy as it looks!)

Passare alle vie di fatto: To follow hostile words with violent action.
LIT. To pass on to ways of deeds.

> Dopo una discussione molto vivace, *son passati alle vie di fatto* e uno di loro è finito all'ospedale. (After a heated argument, they finally came to blows and one of them ended up in the hospital.)

Via crucis: A sequence of painful experiences.
LIT. (Latin for) Road of the cross.

> Dieci anni di matrimonio con quell'uomo devono esser stati una vera *via crucis.* (Ten years of marriage with that man must have been unadulterated hell.)

Via di Damasco*: The road to reforming one's ways.
LIT. Damascus road.

> Mi sembra che abbia preso la *via di Damasco.* (I think he's finally seen the error of his ways.)

Via via che (See also **Mano a mano che**): As, while, in the process of.
LIT. Way way that.

VIAGGIARE To travel

Viaggiare col cavallo di San Francesco: To go on foot, to walk.

---

* Referring to St. Paul's conversion.

LIT. To travel with St. Francis' horse.

Viaggiare in un baule: To travel without really seeing anything.
LIT. To travel in a trunk.

VIAGGIO (IL) Trip

Fare un viaggio e due servizi (See also **Prendere due piccioni**): To kill two birds with one stone.
LIT. To make one trip and two services.

VINCERE To win

Darla vinta a qualcuno: To yield to insistent requests; to give in to someone.
LIT. To give it won to someone.

Darsi per vinto: To give up.
LIT. To give oneself for defeated.

Non si dà mai per vinto. (He never takes no for an answer.)

Vincere un terno al lotto: To hit the jackpot.
LIT. To win a tern at the "lotto" (Italian national lottery).

VINO (IL) Wine

Avere il vino triste: To be the kind of person who gets sad when he drinks.
LIT. To have the sad wine.

Domandare all'oste se il vino è buono (See **Oste**)

In vino veritas
LIT. (Latin for) In wine truth.

Eh no, troppo tardi, mio caro! *In vino veritas.* (Oh, no, my friend, it's too late! The cat's out of the bag.)

Metter dell'acqua nel proprio vino: To climb down from an intransigent or belligerent position.
LIT. To put water in one's own wine.

Ha parlato bene; ma io ricordo i suoi articoli di qualche anno fa. *Ne ha messa d'acqua nel suo vino!* (It was a good speech, but I remember the articles he used to write a few years ago. Has he tamed down since then!)

Nelle botti piccole c'è il vino buono: Good things come in small packages.
LIT. In small casks there is good wine.

VIRTÙ (LA) Virtue

Far di necessità virtù: To make a virtue of necessity.

VISIBILIO (IL) Profusion

Andare in visibilio: To go into raptures.
LIT. To go in profusion (of emotions).

Mandare in visibilio: To throw into raptures.

VISO (IL)

A viso aperto: Frankly; without fear or shame.
LIT. At open face.

Far buon viso a cattivo giuoco (See **Giuoco**)

VISTA (LA) Sight, vision

Leggere a prima vista: To sight-read.
LIT. To read at first sight.

VITA (LA) Life

Dare la mala vita a qualcuno: To be after someone; to pester him.
LIT. To give the bad life to someone.

Mi ha dato la mala vita perché le comprassi una pelliccia, e ora non se la mette mai. (She's been after me for years to buy her a fur coat, and now that she has it she never wears it.)

Fare la vita: To have an exciting social life; to move in fashionable circles; to lead a dissolute life.

LIT. To do the life.

Fare la vita di Michelaccio: To lead the life of Riley.
LIT. To do the life of Michelaccio.

Mors tua vita mea: One man's meat is another man's poison.
LIT. (Latin for) Your death my life.

Passare a miglior vita: To die.
LIT. To pass to better life.

Saper vita morte e miracoli di qualcuno: To know someone like a book.
LIT. To know life, death and miracles of someone.

Vita da non morir mai: Wonderful, great life.
LIT. Life worthy of never dying.

Che delizia, queste vacanze! Una *vita da non morir mai.* (What a vacation! I'd like to live this way forever.)

Vita natural durante: For the rest of one's life.
LIT. While natural life lasts.

E io dovrei sorbirmi i capricci di quella donna *vita natural durante?* Fossi pazzo! (I should put up with that woman's whims for the rest of my life? You think I'm nuts?)

VITTORIA (LA) Victory

Cantar vittoria: To rejoice in an achievement.
LIT. To sing victory.

È troppo presto per *cantar vittoria.* (It's too soon to celebrate.)

Vittoria di Pirro: Pyrrhic victory; a victory that leaves the victor weaker than the vanquished.

VIVERE To live

Lasciarsi vivere: To relax; to take things as they come.
LIT. To let oneself live.

Ho deciso di non prendermela di nulla e di *lasciarmi*

vivere. (I've decided to stop worrying and to take life easy.)

Modus vivendi: Compromise.
LIT. (Latin for) Way of living.

Perfettamente felici magari non saranno, ma almeno hanno trovato *un modus vivendi.* (They may not be idyllically happy, but they have at least found a way to get along.)

Saper vivere: To know how to handle people; to know how to get one's way without hurting people's feelings.
LIT. To know (how) to live.

VIVERI (I) Food, supplies

Tagliare i viveri: To cut someone off without a cent.
LIT. To cut supplies.

VIVO Alive

Farsi vivo: To show up, to drop in.
LIT. To make oneself alive.

Fatti vivo qualche volta! (Let me hear from you every once in a while.)

Pungere qualcuno sul vivo: To hurt someone's feelings; to arouse someone's pride with painful, if deserved, criticism.
LIT. To prick someone on the raw.

Quando hai parlato di apatia politica, ho visto che *l'avevi punto sul vivo.* (When you mentioned political apathy, I thought he looked cut to the quick.)

Vivo e vegeto: Alive and kicking; hale and hearty.
LIT. Alive and thriving.

VOCE (LA) Voice

Aver voce in capitolo: To have a voice in the matter; to have a say.
LIT. To have voice in the chapter (ecclesiastical).

Mi vogliono bene, ma quando si tratta dei bambini *non ho voce in capitolo.* (They love me, of course, but when it comes to the children I'm supposed to keep my opinions to myself.)

Corre voce: Rumor has it.
LIT. Voice runs.

Dar voce: To spread the word.
LIT. To give voice.

Dar sulla voce a qualcuno: To reprimand someone, to call him back to order.
LIT. To give on the voice to someone.

Dare una voce a qualcuno: To give someone a shout; to call someone.
LIT. To give a voice to someone.

Darsi la voce: To pass the word around.
LIT. To give each other the voice.

Si devono *essere dati la voce,* perché nessuno di loro è venuto alla riunione. (They must have planned it that way ahead of time, because none of them showed up at the meeting.)

Fare la voce grossa: To talk sternly.
LIT. To make the big voice.

Con certa gente, se non *si fa la voce grossa,* non si ottiene niente. (With some people, you have to get mad or you don't get anywhere.)

Vox populi vox dei.
LIT. (Latin for) Voice of the people, voice of God.

Vedi che avevo ragione? *Vox populi* . . . (Do you believe me now? Everyone seems to feel the same way.)

VOGLIA (LA) Wish, desire

Aver voglia di: To feel like.
LIT. To have wish to.

Morir dalla voglia di: To be dying to.
LIT. To be dying from the wish to.

Passar la voglia: To lose the desire.
LIT. To pass the wish.

> Dopo tanto discutere, *me n'è passata la voglia.* (After arguing about it so long, I feel like forgetting the whole thing.)

Venir la voglia: To suddenly feel like.
LIT. To come the wish.

> Dopo averlo sentito parlare, *mi è venuta la voglia* di andare a Cape Cod. (Hearing him talk suddenly made me feel like going to Cape Cod.)

VOLO (IL) Flight

A volo: Immediately, rapidly.
LIT. At flight.

> È uno che capisce *a volo.* (He can take a hint—he's very quick on the uptake.)

A volo d'uccello: As the crow flies.
LIT. At flight of bird.

Prendere il volo: To disappear; to flee.
LIT. To take the flight.

VOLPE (LA) Fox

Come la volpe e l'uva: Sour grapes!
LIT. Like the fox and the grapes.

Essere una volpe, essere una volpe vecchia: To be foxy; to be an old fox.

VOLTA (LA) Turn, return, time

A volta di corriere: By return mail; immediately.
LIT. At courier's turning.

Z

ZAMPA (LA) Paw, leg, foot, claw (of an animal, bird, or insect)

Cavar le castagne dal fuoco con la zampa del gatto (See **Gatto**)

Mettere lo zampino in una cosa: To influence matters behind the scenes.
LIT. To put one's little paw into something.

Dì la verità che *ci hai messo lo zampino tu!* (Tell the truth! You had something to do with it!)

Zampa di leone: The mark of genius.
LIT. Lion's paw.

È un romanzo forse un po' faragginoso, ma ci si vede *la zampa del leone*. (As a novel it may be overlong, but it certainly has the mark of genius.)

Zampe di gallina: Crow's feet; bad handwriting; scrawls. LIT. Chicken's feet.

ZIZZANIA (LA) Weeds

Spargere zizzania: To cause friction; to start trouble. LIT. To spread weeds.

WITHDRAWAL